BBC goodfood
SLOW COOKER
FAVOURITES

D1336091

20

First published in 2011 by BBC Books, an imprint of Ebury Publishing
A Random House Group company. This revised edition published 2014.

Photographs © BBC Worldwide 2011, except pages 11, 17, 23, 51, 63, 79, 93, 95, 107, 113, 121, 127, 139, 163
and 193 © Woodlands Books Ltd 2011
Recipes © BBC Worldwide 2011
Book design © Woodlands Books Ltd 2014
All recipes contained in this book first appeared in their original form in BBC Good Food magazine.

The Random House Group Limited. Reg. No. 954009

Addresses for companies within the Random House Group can be found at www.randomhouse.co.uk

A CIP catalogue record for this book is available from the British Library

Penguin Random House is committed to a sustainable future for our business,
our readers and our planet. This book is made from Forest Stewardship
Council® certified paper.

MIX
Paper from
responsible sources
FSC® C018179

To buy books by your favourite authors and register for offers visit www.randomhouse.co.uk

Printed and bound by Firmengruppe APPL, aprinta druck, Wemding, Germany
Colour origination by Dot Gradations Ltd, UK

Edited by Cassie Best
Commissioning Editor: Lizzy Gray
Project Editor: Lizzy Gaisford
Designers: Interstate Creative Partners Ltd
Design Manager: Kathryn Gammon
Production: Alex Goddard
Picture Researcher: Gabby Harrington

ISBN: 9781849908696

PICTURE CREDITS

BBC Good Food magazine and BBC Books would like to thank the following people for providing photos. While every effort has
been made to trace and acknowledge all photographers, we should like to apologise should there be any errors or omissions.

Marie-Louise Avery p209; John Bennett p65; Peter Cassidy p191; Jean Cazals p181, p199; Ken Field p119; Will Heap p21, p27, p91,
p161, p165, p175; Gareth Morgans p13, p17, p23, p41, p51, p63, p73, p79, p81, p87, p93, p95, p97, p107, p113, p121, p127, p139,
p149, p151, p153, p163, p179, p193; David Munns p15, p43, p45, p47, p53, p59, p67, p75, p109, p115, p117, p123, p129, p133,
p137, p143, p173, p185, p187, p197; Myles New p31, p33, p69, p71, p83, p99, p101, p141, p155, p171, p203; Lis Parsons p11, p19,
p29, p35, p37, p39, p49, p89, p103, p131, p145, p147, p157, p167, p195, p205, p211; Sam Stowell p25, p55, p65, p111, p169; Simon
Walton p183; Ian Wallace p207; Philip Webb p57, p61, p77, p85, p105, p135, p177, p189, p201;

All the recipes in this book were created by the editorial team at Good Food and by regular contributors to BBC Magazines.

SLOW COOKER
FAVOURITES

Editor **Sarah Cook**

BOOKS

Contents

· ·

Introduction
. . . .

Slow cookers are making a comeback because they're a fantastic way to create delicious home-cooked meals with very little effort. Fuss-free and incredibly energy efficient, they're also the perfect way to make the most of cheap cuts of meat – but don't think that's where their advantages end...

From soups to sweet things – and even pasta bakes – slow cookers are as versatile as they are easy to use, which is why we've put together this book with more than just stews in mind. We've taken some of our favourite *Good Food* recipes and adapted and tested them in our kitchen so they'll really work in your slow cooker, and this revised and updated edition has the best of them all. Plus, whether you're looking for a home-from-work supper that you throw together at breakfast time, a way to effortlessly entertain, or simply something

tasty that'll look after itself while you get on with other things, you'll find a wide variety from which to choose in this brilliant little book.

Not only will you discover recipes with a bit of a difference, but you'll also find all of the classics from chilli con carne to chicken casserole. Whatever you're after, you'll get it here – including all the slow-cooking tips we've picked up along the way.

So now all that's left is for you to plug in and get started. Slow cookers are back!

Sarah

Sarah Cook
BBC *Good Food* magazine

Notes &
Conversion Tables
. . . .

GETTING THE BEST FROM YOUR SLOW COOKER

Every slow cooker is different, so make sure you keep your manufacturer's manual handy when using it. However, here we'll share with you the *Good Food* team's top tips for slow cooking.

- Lots of the recipes can be changed to fit in with your lifestyle, so follow your manual's guidelines on decreasing or increasing cooking times by changing the temperature of the slow cooker. However, we've found rice and pasta dishes really work best when cooked on High for the shortest time possible.
- Always use easy-cook rice, if you can get it, and don't forget to rinse the rice well first. The more starch you can wash off the rice, the better the finished dish.
- Slow cookers vary considerably in size, so we've written a variety of recipes, for a variety of portions. Many of these are easily halved or doubled – check the individual recipes for recommendations.

- If the sauce of a stew or a casserole is a little thin for your liking, mix 1 tablespoon cornflour to a paste with a splash of the sauce, then transfer to a pan with a ladleful of the sauce and bring to the boil to thicken. Stir back into the stew and repeat if need be.
- If you want to adapt your own recipes to suit a slow cooker, look for something similar in this book and copy the timings – but reduce the liquid in your original recipe by around a third.

Notes on the recipes
- Eggs are large in the UK and Australia and extra large in America unless stated.
- Wash fresh produce before preparation.
- Recipes contain nutritional analyses for 'sugar', which means the total sugar content including all natural sugars.

SPOON MEASURES

Spoon measurements are level unless otherwise specified.

- 1 teaspoon (tsp) = 5ml
- 1 tablespoon (tbsp) = 15ml
- 1 Australian tablespoon = 20ml (cooks in Australia should measure 3 teaspoons where 1 tablespoon is specified in a recipe)

APPROXIMATE LIQUID CONVERSIONS

METRIC	IMPERIAL	AUS	US
50ml	2fl oz	¼ cup	¼ cup
125ml	4fl oz	½ cup	½ cup
175ml	6fl oz	¾ cup	¾ cup
225ml	8fl oz	1 cup	1 cup
300ml	10fl oz/½ pint	½ pint	1¼ cups
450ml	16fl oz	2 cups	2 cups/1 pint
600ml	20fl oz/1 pint	1 pint	2½ cups
1 litre	35fl oz/1¾ pints	1¾ pints	1 quart

APPROXIMATE WEIGHT CONVERSIONS

- All the recipes in this book list both imperial and metric measurements. Conversions are approximate and have been rounded up or down. Follow one set of measurements only; do not mix.
- Cup measurements, which are used in Australia and America, have not been listed here as they vary from ingredient to ingredient. Kitchen scales should be used to measure dry/solid ingredients.

Good Food is concerned about sustainable sourcing and animal welfare. Where possible, humanely reared meats, sustainably caught fish (see fishonline.org for further information from the Marine Conservation Society) and free-range chickens and eggs are used when recipes are originally tested.

Better-than-baked beans

. . . .

Prepare this the night before and you'll wake up to hot homemade baked beans, perfect with lots of buttered toast, plus bacon, sausages or fried eggs, if you wish.

 10–11 hours 4 Easily halved or doubled

- 2 tsp oil
- 2 onions, halved and thinly sliced
- 4 rashers streaky bacon, cut into large-ish pieces
- 2 tsp brown sugar
- 2 x 400g cans chopped tomatoes
- 200ml/7fl oz stock from a cube
- 2 x 410g cans cannellini, butter or haricot beans in water, drained and rinsed
- buttered toast, to serve

1 Heat the slow cooker if necessary. Heat the oil in a non-stick pan, then gently fry the onions and bacon together for 5–10 minutes until the onions are softened and just starting to turn golden. Stir in the sugar, tomatoes, stock and some seasoning to taste, then simmer the sauce for 5 minutes.

2 Tip everything into the slow-cooker pot and stir in the beans. Cover with the lid and cook on Low overnight or for 9–10 hours.

3 Stir well and serve on buttered toast.

. . . .

PER SERVING 263 kcals, protein 16g, carbs 35g, fat 8g, sat fat 2g, fibre 10g, sugar 13g, salt 1.37g

Apple, pear & cherry compote

This is worth making in a big batch, as it will last all week in the fridge and it also freezes brilliantly.

 8-10 hours   8-12   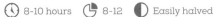 Easily halved

- 8 eating apples, peeled, cored and cut into chunks
- 4 Bramley apples, peeled, cored and cut into chunks
- 8 firm pears, peeled, cored and thickly sliced
- 6 tbsp sugar, or to taste
- 300g/10oz dried sour cherries (or dried cranberries)
- pancakes, yogurt or cereal, to serve

1 Heat the slow cooker if necessary. Put the apples, pears, sugar and cherries (or cranberries) into the slow-cooker pot with 50ml/2fl oz water, and give everything a really good stir. Cover and cook on Low overnight, or for up to 8–10 hours, until the Bramley apples have collapsed to a purée and the eating apples and pears are tender.
2 Eat hot, at room temperature or cold, with pancakes, yogurt or cereal.

PER SERVING (8) 199 kcals, protein 1g, carbs 51g, fat 1g, sat fat none, fibre 4g, sugar 47g, salt 0.03g

Honey-crunch granola

This might seem an unusual dish to make in the slow cooker, but it really works – see for yourself!

 2 hours, plus cooling   14

- 125ml/4fl oz sunflower oil
- 100ml/3½fl oz malt extract
- 100ml/3½fl oz clear honey
- 250g/9oz rolled oats
- 250g/9oz jumbo oats
- 25g/1oz desiccated coconut
- 50g/2oz sunflower seeds
- 25g/1oz sesame seeds
- 140g/5oz whole brazil nuts
- 100g/4oz mixed dried fruit (such as sultanas, chopped apricots or dates)

1 Heat the slow cooker if necessary. Put in the oil, malt extract and honey, and cook on High for 30 minutes, without a cover, until the malt extract becomes runny. Stir, then add the remaining ingredients, except the brazil nuts and dried fruit, and stir until evenly coated.

2 Turn the cooker to Low and cook, covered, for 45 minutes, then remove the lid, stir, and cook for 30 minutes more until crisp. Tip out into a baking tin or a bowl to cool and stir in the brazil nuts and fruit. Once cool, transfer to a jar or other airtight container and keep for up to a month.

PER SERVING 591 kcals, protein 12g, carbs 63g, fat 34g, sat fat 7g, fibre 6g, sugar 24g, salt 0.04g

Tomato baked eggs

You can prepare this in the evening, let it cook all night, then simply add the eggs in the morning to finish.

 10 hours 4  easily halved

- 900g/2lb ripe vine tomatoes
- 3 garlic cloves, thinly sliced
- 3 tbsp olive oil
- 4 eggs
- 2 tbsp chopped flat-leaf parsley or snipped chives
- buttered toast, to serve

1 Heat the slow cooker if necessary. Cut the tomatoes into quarters or thick wedges, depending on their size, then tip them into the slow-cooker pot. Sprinkle over the garlic, drizzle with the olive oil and season well with salt and pepper. Stir everything together.
2 Cover with the lid and cook on Low overnight or for 9 hours.
3 Make four dips among the tomatoes and crack an egg into each. Re-cover with the lid and cook on High for 30 minutes until the whites are set and the yolks are cooked to your liking. Scatter with the parsley or chives and serve with buttered toast.

PER SERVING 204 kcals, protein 9g, carbs 7g, fat 16g, sat fat 3g, fibre 3g, sugar none, salt 0.27g

Apple & spice tea loaf

This loaf looks as good as anything you might pick up at a cake shop or farmers' market, and tastes spicy, fruity and light.

 4 hours   10

- 175g/6oz butter, plus extra for greasing and to serve
- 175g/6oz light muscovado sugar, plus 1 tsp
- 3 eggs, beaten
- 1 eating apple
- 1 tsp vanilla extract
- 200g/8oz dried mixed vine fruits
- 85g/3oz ground almonds
- 1 tsp each baking powder and ground cinnamon
- ½ tsp ground nutmeg
- 175g/6oz plain flour
- splash lemon or orange juice
- 1 tbsp marmalade or apricot jam

1 Heat the slow cooker if necessary, with an upturned saucer in the bottom. Butter a 1kg loaf tin and line with baking paper, or use a liner. Beat together the butter and sugar until pale, then beat in the eggs one by one. Grate half the apple and mix in with the vanilla, dried fruit and almonds. Mix the baking powder, spices and flour together with a pinch of salt, then fold into the mix until even. Spoon into the tin and level the top.

2 Thinly slice the remaining apple half, toss with the lemon or orange juice, poke the slices a little way into the batter, then sprinkle with the extra teaspoon of the sugar. Put in the slow cooker, cover with the lid and bake on High for 2–3 hours until a skewer poked into the centre comes out clean. Cool in the tin.

3 To finish the cake, melt the marmalade or jam in a small pan, then brush it over the loaf to glaze the top. Serve in slices, spread with a little butter.

PER SLICE 416 kcals, protein 7g, carbs 50g, fat 22g, sat fat 10g, fibre 2g, sugar 36g, salt 0.54g

Slow-cooked porridge

. . . .

Put this oaty breakfast into your slow cooker before you go to bed and wake up to a bowl of creamy comfort in the morning.

🕐 5 minutes, plus overnight cooking   🍴 4

- 1 cup jumbo oats
- 4 cups milk (or half milk, half water for a less creamy version), plus dribble more milk to loosen
- ¼ cup mixed dried fruit (optional)

TO SERVE
- your favourite toppings – brown sugar or honey, sliced bananas, grated apple, blueberries, pinch ground cinnamon, natural yogurt, etc.

1 Heat the slow cooker if necessary. Put the oats in a heat-proof bowl along with a pinch of salt, then pour over the milk, or a mixture of milk and water. Add the dried fruit, if using. Put the bowl in the slow cooker, turn it to its lowest setting and cook overnight for 7–8 hours. If anyone's up in the night, get them to give the porridge a quick stir to scrape up the crustier bits from around the edges and bottom, but it's not essential.

2 In the morning, give the porridge a really good stir – it may have developed a crust on top, but just stir to break it up. Add a drop more milk to loosen if necessary, then ladle into bowls and add your favourite toppings.

. . . .
PER SERVING 264 kcals, protein 15g, carbs 33g, fat 7g, sat fat 3g, fibre 4g, sugar 11g, salt 0.4g

Herby bean–sausage stew

This is a great breakfast, which can be easily varied to suit your tastes: swap the herbs for Worcestershire sauce or add some chopped bacon or sliced mushrooms.

 8½ hours   4   Easily halved or doubled

- 8 chipolatas
- 2 x 400g cans mixed beans, drained and rinsed
- 2 x 400g cans chopped tomatoes
- 1 tsp dried basil
- 2 tsp dried oregano
- 1 tbsp sugar
- buttered toast, to serve (optional)

1 Heat the slow cooker if necessary. Heat a large non-stick frying pan, then brown the sausages for 3–5 minutes over a high heat. Transfer to the slow-cooker pot with the beans. Add one can of tomatoes, then drain the contents of the other can through a sieve discarding the juice and just adding the chopped tomatoes to the pot. Stir in the basil, oregano and sugar with some seasoning, then cover and cook on Low overnight or for up to 8 hours.

2 Check for seasoning, then serve in bowls or on buttered toast, if you like.

PER SERVING 355 kcals, protein 20g, carbs 37g, fat 15g, sat fat 5g, fibre 10g, sugar 13g, salt 2.68g

Pesto & mozzarella-stuffed mushrooms

. . . .

Italian green basil and pine-nut sauce and creamy mascarpone make a good base for this stuffed, vegetarian dish, simply served with a light rocket salad.

🕐 3 hours 10 minutes   🍽 2

- 2 tbsp olive oil, plus extra for greasing
- 1 onion, chopped
- 4 large Portobello mushrooms, stalks finely chopped
- 100g/4oz light mascarpone
- zest and juice ½ lemon
- 4 tbsp basil pesto
- 125g ball light mozzarella, chopped
- 25g/1oz dried breadcrumbs
- large handful rocket leaves
- 100g/4oz cherry tomatoes, halved

1 Heat half the oil in a small pan and cook the onion and chopped mushroom stalks for 5–8 minutes until soft. Tip into a bowl, allow to cool slightly, then add the mascarpone, lemon zest, pesto, mozzarella and seasoning.

2 Heat the slow cooker to High. Grease the inside of the slow cooker with a little oil, add the whole mushrooms, in a single layer. Divide the stuffing among the mushrooms, spreading to fill the middle of each one. Top each with breadcrumbs and a grind of black pepper, then cover with the lid and cook for 3 hours until the mushrooms are tender. If you want to crisp the tops, heat grill to high, slide the mushrooms on to a baking sheet and cook for a few minutes, until golden.

3 Meanwhile, make the dressing. Whisk the remaining oil with the lemon juice and some seasoning. Dress the rocket leaves and tomatoes and serve with the mushrooms.

. . . .

PER SERVING 560 kcals, protein 30g, carbs 24g, fat 38g, sat fat 12g, fibre 6g, sugar 13g, salt 1.8g

Spiced carrot & lentil soup

If you've got a very large slow cooker it's worth making a double batch of this low-fat, superhealthy soup as it freezes beautifully for up to 3 months.

 4 hours · 4 · Easily doubled

- 2 tsp cumin seeds
- pinch dried chilli flakes
- 2 tbsp olive oil
- 600g/1lb 5oz carrots, washed and coarsely grated (no need to peel)
- 140g/5oz red split lentils
- 700ml/1¼ pints hot vegetable stock
- 125ml/4fl oz milk
- natural yogurt and warmed naan bread, to serve

1 Heat the slow cooker if necessary. Put half the cumin seeds, half the chilli flakes, the oil, carrots, lentils and stock in the slow-cooker pot. Cover and cook on High for 3 hours until the lentils are tender.

2 Dry-fry the remaining cumin seeds and chilli flakes just until fragrant.

3 When the lentils are done, stir in the milk and whizz the soup with a stick blender or in a food processor until smooth (or leave it chunky, if you prefer). Add a splash of water if the soup is a bit thick for you. Season to taste and finish with a dollop of yogurt and a sprinkling of the toasted spices. Serve with warmed naan bread.

PER SERVING 238 kcals, protein 11g, carbs 34g, fat 7g, sat fat 1g, fibre 5g, sugar none, salt 0.25g

Country terrine with black pepper & thyme
. . . .

This may seem an unusual dish to cook in a slow cooker, but it's a brilliant way to stop the meat drying out.

🕐 5 hours, plus overnight chilling   🍽 8

- butter, for greasing
- 750g/1lb 10oz rashers pork belly
- 1 tbsp dried thyme
- 1 tsp black peppercorns
- 2 x 225g tubs frozen chicken livers, thawed
- 4 tbsp red or white wine (optional)
- 5 rashers smoked streaky bacon
- cocktail gherkins or chutney, and toast or bread, to serve

1 Heat the slow cooker if necessary and butter a 900g loaf tin. Finely chop three of the pork-belly rashers and mix with the thyme and peppercorns. Blend the remaining pork belly in a food processor with two-thirds of the chicken livers, the wine (if using) and 1 teaspoon salt, to make a smooth pâté.
2 Spoon half the pâté into the loaf tin, then top with the chopped-pork mixture and remaining livers. Spoon over the rest of the pâté, then lay the bacon on top.
3 Cover the tin with foil and put in the slow cooker. Add boiling water to the cooker pot halfway up the sides of the tin. Cover and bake on High for 3–4 hours until firm and the juices run clear when poked with a skewer. Drain off any liquid in the tin. Cool, then put another loaf tin on top and weight it down with cans. Chill overnight before slicing and serving with gherkins or chutney and toast or bread.

. . . .
PER SERVING 330 kcals, protein 30g, carbs none, fat 23g, sat fat 9g, fibre none, sugar none, salt 0.64g

Sweetcorn & smoked-haddock chowder

The perfect lunch for two, just add some fresh crusty bread and butter, and let the slow cooker do most of the work.

 4 hours 2 Easily doubled

- knob butter
- 2 rashers streaky bacon, chopped
- 1 onion, finely chopped
- 350g/12oz potatoes, cut into small cubes
- 500ml/18fl oz whole milk
- 140g/5oz sweetcorn, frozen or from a can
- 300g/10oz smoked haddock fillets, skinned
- chopped parsley, to garnish (optional)
- crusty bread, to serve

1 Heat the slow cooker if necessary. Heat the butter in a frying pan. Tip in the bacon, onion and potatoes, then fry gently until the onion is soft. Scrape the bacon mix into the slow-cooker pot with the milk. Cover and cook on High for 3 hours until the potatoes are tender.

2 Stir in the sweetcorn, sit the fish fillets on top and press down so they sit just under the surface of the liquid. Cover and cook for another 20–30 minutes until the fish flakes easily when pressed.

3 Turn off the slow-cooker pot and carefully lift the fish out and on to a plate. Flake into large chunks, checking for bones and discarding them as you go. Gently stir the fish back into the chowder, season with some black pepper, and check the seasoning in case you need to add any salt. Scatter over the parsley, if using, and serve with plenty of crusty bread.

PER SERVING 550 kcals, protein 47g, carbs 59g, fat 16g, sat fat 7g, fibre 4g, sugar 18g, salt 3.92g

Split pea & green pea smoked-ham soup

. . . .

You can easily make this soup ahead, then simply return it to the slow cooker and heat through for an hour on High until piping hot but not bubbling.

 5-6 hours, plus overnight soaking 8 Easily halved

- 1kg/2lb 4oz ham hock
- 200g/8oz split peas, soaked overnight
- 2 onions, roughly chopped
- 2 carrots, roughly chopped
- 2 bay leaves
- 1 celery stick, roughly chopped
- 300g/10oz frozen peas
- crusty bread and butter, to serve

1 Put the ham in a large pan with 2 litres/3½ pints water and bring to the boil. Remove from the heat and drain off the water.

2 Heat the slow cooker if necessary. Add the ham to the pot with the cooking water, split peas, onion, carrots, bay and celery. Cover with the lid and cook on High for 4–5 hours until the ham is tender enough to shred – testing it occasionally. You can halve it if you want, so it is all submerged under the liquid.

3 When it is ready, remove the ham to a plate and discard the bay leaves, then tip the frozen peas into the slow cooker. Cook for another 30 minutes while you prepare the ham. Peel off and discard the skin, and while it is still hot (wear a clean pair of rubber gloves), shred the meat. Blend the soup until smooth, adding a splash of water if too thick, and then mix in most of the ham. Serve in bowls with the remaining ham scattered on top, and eat with crusty bread and butter.

. . . .

PER SERVING 292 kcals, protein 26g, carbs 23g, fat 11g, sat fat 4g, fibre 5g, sugar 5g, salt 3.56g

Salsa-chicken peppers

These peppers make a lovely lunch with an avocado or a green salad and are a great way to use up any leftover chicken from dinner the night before.

 3 hours   4–6    Easily halved

- 140g/5oz Camargue red rice or brown basmati rice
- 6 large red peppers
- oil, for brushing
- 270g jar hot salsa
- 200g/8oz cooked chicken, chopped
- 215g can red kidney beans, drained and rinsed
- 40g/1½oz mature Cheddar, grated
- 20g pack coriander leaves, chopped
- lime wedges, to garnish
- avocado salad, to serve

1 Boil the rice for 25 minutes, or according to the pack instructions, until just tender. Meanwhile, heat the slow cooker if necessary. Slice the tops off the peppers and cut out and discard the seeds. Set aside the peppers and their tops. Oil the base of the slow-cooker pot.

2 Drain the rice and mix with the salsa, chicken, beans, Cheddar and coriander. Season to taste. Fill the peppers with the rice mixture. Put on the tops, then sit the stuffed peppers in the slow cooker and cover with the lid. Cook for 2 hours on High until the peppers are tender. Serve with lime wedges to squeeze over and an avocado salad.

PER SERVING (4) 370 kcals, protein 24g, carbs 50g, fat 10g, sat fat 4g, fibre 5g, sugar 15g, salt 1.65g

Roast chicken soup

Make this with leftovers from the Sunday roast, or simply poach a couple of chicken breasts in the slow cooker first, following the manufacturer's instructions.

 5 hours 4

- 1 tbsp olive oil
- 2 onions, chopped
- 3 medium carrots, chopped
- 1 tbsp thyme leaves, roughly chopped
- 1 litre/1¾ pints chicken stock
- 300g/10oz leftover roast chicken, shredded, or 1 chicken carcass
- 200g/8oz frozen peas
- 3 tbsp Greek yogurt
- 1 garlic clove, crushed
- squeeze lemon juice
- crusty bread, to serve

1 Heat the slow cooker if necessary and heat the oil in a large heavy-based pan. Add the onions, carrots and thyme, then gently fry for 15 minutes. Tip the veg into the slow-cooker pot with the stock. If you're using a chicken carcass, add it now, breaking it in half if you need to. Cover and cook for 2–3 hours on High until the vegetables are tender.

2 If you used a carcass, remove it now, and shred any remaining chicken off the bones. Stir this back into the soup, or add your leftover shredded chicken now, if using that instead, plus the peas, and cover and cook for 30 minutes more.

3 Remove half the mixture, then purée with a stick blender (or ladle half the mixture into a blender or food processor and purée that). Tip back into the pot and season to taste.

4 Mix the yogurt, garlic and lemon juice, swirl into the soup in bowls, then serve with some crusty bread.

PER SERVING 339 kcals, protein 39g, carbs 18g, fat 13g, sat fat 3g, fibre 6g, sugar 11g, salt 2.00g

Easy cheese fondue

Using mild cheese in this recipe means everyone can enjoy it, but if you fancy just making this for grown-ups you can swap the Cheddar for something with more bite.

 1¼ hours 6–8

- 2 tbsp cider vinegar
- 1 tsp cornflour
- 3 tbsp crème fraîche
- 250g/9oz Cheddar, grated
- 250g/9oz Gruyère, grated

SUGGESTIONS FOR DIPPING

- 4 thick slices bread, toasted, in chunks
- 2 carrots, cut into batons
- 2 peppers, deseeded and cut into strips
- 2 celery sticks, thickly sliced
- 200g/8oz mini salamis or 1 thin salami, cut into bite-sized chunks

1 Heat the slow cooker if necessary. Mix the vinegar with the cornflour, then stir in the crème fraîche. Scatter the cheeses into the slow-cooker pot then dot the crème fraîche mixture on top. Cover and cook on High for 1 hour, stirring halfway, until the cheeses have melted.

2 Season the fondue with black pepper and give it a good whisk. Then serve it with your favourites for dipping in.

PER SERVING (6) 374 kcals, protein 22g, carbs 1g, fat 31g, sat fat 20g, fibre none, sugar none, salt 1.48g

Rich tomato soup with pesto

This soup cleverly uses canned tomatoes, so there's no reason not to enjoy homemade tomato soup even in the depths of winter.

 6 hours 4

- 1 tbsp olive oil
- 2 garlic cloves, crushed
- 5 soft sun-dried or SunBlush tomatoes in oil, drained and roughly chopped
- 3 x 400g cans plum tomatoes
- 250ml/9fl oz vegetable stock
- 1 tsp sugar, any type, or more to taste
- 150ml pot soured cream
- 125g/4½ oz fresh basil pesto
- basil leaves, to garnish

1 Heat the slow cooker if necessary. Put the olive oil, garlic, dried tomatoes, canned tomatoes, stock and sugar in the slow-cooker pot. Cover and cook on Low for 4–5 hours until the onion is soft.

2 Add half of the soured cream and purée the soup while still in the pot with a stick blender, or ladle into a blender or food processor in batches to purée. Taste and adjust the seasoning – adding more sugar, along with some salt and black pepper, if you need to. Serve in bowls with 1 tablespoon or so of the pesto swirled on top, a little more soured cream and a scattering of basil leaves.

PER SERVING 213 kcals, protein 8g, carbs 14g, fat 14g, sat fat 7g, fibre 4g, sugar 13g, salt 1.15g

Chicken tikka masala

. . . .

 3 hours  10 Easily halved

This curry is so delicious you'll make it time and again. You can make your own paste, but it is still tasty made with shop-bought versions. Serve with rice and naan bread.

- 4 onions, roughly chopped
- 25g/1oz butter
- 4 tbsp vegetable oil
- 6 tbsp tikka masala curry paste (or use recipe below)
- 2 red peppers, deseeded and cut into chunks
- 8 boneless skinless chicken breasts, cut into chunks
- 2 x 400g cans chopped tomatoes
- 4 tbsp tomato purée
- 2–3 tbsp mango chutney
- 150ml/¼ pint each double cream and natural yogurt
- chopped coriander, to garnish

FOR HOMEMADE CURRY PASTE
- 5 garlic cloves
- large knob ginger
- 1 red chilli
- 2 tsp each ground cumin, coriander, turmeric and garam masala

1 If making your own paste, roughly chop the garlic and ginger, deseed and roughly chop the chilli, then whizz together all the paste ingredients with a splash of water.

2 Heat the slow cooker if necessary. Fry the onions in the butter and oil for 5–10 minutes until soft. Add the curry paste and peppers, then fry for 5 minutes more. Add the chicken, stirring to coat in the paste and cook for 2 minutes more. Tip in the tomatoes, purée and 200ml/7fl oz water, and bring to a simmer.

3 Transfer to the slow-cooker pot and push the chicken below the liquid. Cover and cook on High for 2 hours.

4 Stir in the chutney, cream and yogurt, re-cover and cook for another 15–30 minutes until hot through. Scatter with coriander to serve.

. . . .

PER SERVING 345 kcals, protein 31g, carbs 13g, fat 19g, sat fat 8g, fibre 3g, sugar 10g, salt 1.04g

Poule au pot

. . . .

This simple French dish makes a wonderful Sunday lunch for the family.

 6 hours 6

- 1.5 kg/3lb 5oz whole chicken
- 12 small potatoes, peeled
- 300ml/½ pint white wine
- 1 onion, peeled, but left whole and studded with 3 cloves
- 1 bouquet garni
- 3 garlic cloves, unpeeled
- 4 carrots, cut into 5cm/2in lengths
- 2 turnips, cut into wedges
- 200ml tub crème fraîche
- 3 leeks, cut into 5cm/2in lengths
- roughly chopped parsley, to garnish
- stuffing balls, to serve

1 Heat the slow cooker if necessary. Put in the chicken, potatoes, 600ml/1 pint water, the wine, clove-studded onion, bouquet garni, garlic and some seasoning. Cover and cook on High for 3 hours.

2 After 2 hours, fish out and reserve the garlic. Add the carrots and turnips, turn the chicken over then re-cover and cook on High for another 2 hours. Squeeze the garlic cloves out of their skins and mash with some seasoning. Stir into the crème fraîche, then chill until ready to serve.

3 After the second 2 hours of cooking, add the leeks, and cover and cook on High for another hour, at which point the chicken should be done.

4 Lift out the chicken and veg, and reserve one ladle of stock. Pour the rest into a pan and boil to reduce. Remove the chicken's skin and tear the flesh into chunks. Put on a warm platter with the veg and stuffing balls. Add the ladle of stock and the parsley, and serve with the reduced juices and garlic cream.

. . . .

PER SERVING 745 kcals, protein 54g, carbs 48g, fat 37g, sat fat 16g, fibre 7g, sugar 14g, salt 1.31g

One-pan chicken couscous

This ticks all the boxes – it's low fat, needs no accompaniments and any leftovers are perfect packed up for lunch the next day.

 2½ hours   4   Easily halved or doubled

- 1–2 tbsp harissa paste, plus extra to serve (optional)
- 1 tbsp olive oil
- 1 onion, thinly sliced
- good chunk ginger, peeled and grated
- 200g/8oz boneless skinless chicken breast, diced
- 10 dried apricots, halved if you like
- 200ml/7fl oz hot chicken stock
- 220g can chickpeas, drained and rinsed
- 200g/8oz couscous
- handful chopped coriander, to garnish

1 Heat the slow cooker if necessary. Loosen the harissa with the olive oil then put in the slow-cooker pot with the onion and ginger. Cover and cook for 1 hour on High until softened. Add the chicken, apricots and stock, and cook for 1 hour more until the chicken is cooked through.

2 Turn off the slow cooker. Stir in the chickpeas and couscous with some seasoning, cover and set aside for 10 minutes until the couscous is soft. Fluff up the couscous with a fork and scatter with coriander. Serve with extra harissa, if you like.

PER SERVING 281 kcals, protein 20g, carbs 41g, fat 6g, sat fat 1g, fibre 3g, sugar 9g, salt 0.48g

Mexican chicken stew

· ·

Chipotle paste adds a really authentic smoky flavour to this low-fat stew. Serve with rice or corn tortillas.

 2½ hours 4

- 1 tbsp vegetable oil
- 1 medium onion, finely chopped
- 3 garlic cloves, finely chopped
- ½ tsp dark brown sugar
- 1 tsp chipotle paste
- 400g can chopped tomatoes
- 4 skinless chicken breasts
- 1 small red onion, sliced into rings, and a few coriander leaves, to garnish
- rice or corn tortillas, to serve

1 Heat the slow cooker if necessary. Heat the oil in a medium pan, add the onion and cook for 5 minutes or until softened and starting to turn golden, adding the garlic for the final minute. Scrape into the slow-cooker pot and stir in the sugar, chipotle paste, tomatoes and chicken. Cover and cook on High for 2 hours.

2 Remove the chicken from the pot and shred with two forks, then stir the meat back into the sauce – adding a splash of water if the sauce is a little thick. Season, scatter with a few of the red onion slices and the coriander, and serve with the remaining red onion slices and some tortillas or rice.

· ·
PER SERVING 203 kcals, protein 35g, carbs 6g, fat 5g, sat fat 1g, fibre 2g, sugar 4g, salt 0.37g

Saucy chicken & spring vegetables

Add a spoon of grainy mustard to the sauce with the crème fraîche, if you like it tangy.

 3 hours   2

- 2 boneless chicken breasts, skin on
- 1 tbsp olive oil
- 200g/8oz baby new potatoes, thinly sliced
- 250ml/9fl oz chicken stock
- 200g pack mixed spring veg (broccoli, peas, broad beans and sliced courgettes)
- 2 tbsp crème fraîche
- handful tarragon leaves, roughly chopped

1 Heat the slow cooker if necessary. Fry the chicken, skin-side down, in the oil in a frying pan for 5 minutes to brown. Turn the chicken over, throw in the potatoes and stir to coat. Spread the potatoes over the bottom of the slow-cooker pot, then sit the chicken on top. Pour over the stock then cover and cook on High for 1½ hours.

2 Remove the chicken and stir in the veg, then pop the chicken back on top, cover and cook for another hour until the chicken and potatoes are cooked through.

3 Stir in the crème fraîche to make a creamy sauce, season with black pepper and salt, if you want, then add the tarragon. If you like a thicker sauce, scoop out the chicken and veg with a slotted spoon and reduce the sauce by bubbling it in the frying pan.

PER SERVING 386 kcals, protein 38g, carbs 23g, fat 16g, sat fat 6g, fibre 3g, sugar none, salt 1.5g

Chinese roast duck with pancakes

· ·

Cooking Chinese food doesn't have to be complicated when you've got a slow cooker – so let it do the hard work for you and simply finish it quickly under the grill.

 6 hours 4

- 1 oven-ready duck
- 2 tsp Chinese five-spice powder
- 2 star anise
- 1 orange, peel cut off in strips, fruit halved
- 2 tbsp Chinese black vinegar (optional)
- 75ml/2½fl oz Shaohsing rice wine or dry sherry
- 100ml/3½fl oz chicken stock
- 30 Chinese pancakes
- 6 spring onions, cut into finger lengths and shredded, ½ cucumber, cut into matchsticks, and hoisin sauce, to serve

1 Heat the slow cooker if necessary. Loosen the skin on the duck by wriggling first your fingers and then your hand between it and the flesh until it pulls away – be careful not to break the skin. Trim off any excess fat from the cavity and skin around the neck. Rub the skin all over with the five-spice plus a good sprinkling of salt. Push the star anise, orange peel and orange halves inside the cavity, and put the duck in the slow cooker.

2 Spoon over the vinegar, if using, rice wine or sherry and stock. Cover and cook on High for 4–5 hours until very tender. When cooked, flash the duck under a hot grill to crisp up the skin. Let it rest for 10 minutes then shred the meat and skin – you may need to wear gloves to do this as it will be very hot. Heat the pancakes and serve the duck with all of the accompaniments.

· ·

PER SERVING 705 kcals, protein 30g, carbs 42g, fat 46g, sat fat 12g, fibre 3g, sugar 5g, salt 1.08g

Thai green chicken curry

Try this fragrant Thai spice-pot with chicken, green beans, basil and basmati rice.

 2 hours · 2

- 1 tsp vegetable oil
- 1 red onion, cut into half-moon slices
- 4 tbsp Thai green curry paste
- 2 x 400ml cans light coconut milk
- 2 tbsp fish sauce
- zest and juice 2 limes
- 1 tbsp brined green peppercorns, drained and rinsed
- 200g/8oz green beans, trimmed and halved
- 4 boneless skinless chicken breasts, cut into long strips
- handful basil leaves
- cooked basmati rice, to serve

1 Heat the slow cooker if necessary. Heat the oil in a medium pan, add the onion and fry for 2 minutes. Tip in the paste and cook for 1 minute more. Pour in the coconut milk, transfer to the pot of the slow cooker and add the fish sauce, lime zest and juice, peppercorns, beans and chicken. Cook for 1½–2 hours or until the chicken is cooked through.
2 Just before serving, add the basil leaves. Serve with basmati rice.

PER SERVING 352 kcals, protein 35g, carbs 9g, fat 20g, sat fat 13g, fibre 3g, sugar 5g, salt 2.5g

Summer roast chicken

. . . .

The vinaigrette in this dish is a delicious alternative to gravy, making it a perfect dish in the summer when you fancy something lighter than a traditional roast.

 6 hours   4

- 50g/2oz unsalted butter, softened
- juice ½ lemon
- small bunch sage, leaves only, roughly chopped
- 1 whole chicken, about 1.6kg/3lb 8oz
- 1 bulb garlic, broken into cloves in the skins
- 7 tbsp olive oil
- 600g/1lb 5oz small potatoes, scrubbed, cut in half, if large
- 300ml/½ pint chicken stock
- 4 large courgettes, cut into large chunks
- 2 red peppers, halved and deseeded
- 200g/8oz baby plum tomatoes, skin slashed with a knife
- 1 tbsp red wine vinegar

1 Heat the slow cooker if necessary. Mash the butter, lemon juice, sage and some seasoning. Separate the skin from the chicken breast using your hand – being careful not to break the skin. Rub the butter underneath and stuff the cavity with half the garlic. Fry the chicken in 4 tablespoons of the oil in a large frying pan until browned all over. Transfer to the slow-cooker pot breast-side down. Stir the potatoes into the pan, frying until golden, then scrape into the pot too. Add the stock, season then cover and cook on High for 4 hours.

2 Turn the chicken over and add the courgettes, pushing them under the chicken to cover with the stock. Fill the pepper halves with tomatoes and add these to the pot with the remaining garlic. Cover and cook for another hour until the chicken is done. Transfer the chicken and veg to a serving dish to rest, covered with foil. Tip the pot juices into a pan, bubble until reduced by half, stir in remaining oil and the vinegar, and serve.

. . . .

PER SERVING 962 kcals, protein 60g, carbs 36g, fat 65g, sat fat 28g, fibre 5g, sugar 9g, salt 0.73g

Chicken, leek & parsley pie

· ·

If you want to make this pie ahead, prepare the filling and cool it, then top with pastry and freeze. Then just defrost the pie overnight and bake as usual.

 8 hours   4–6

- 1.5kg/3lb 5oz whole chicken
- 1 each carrot, onion and celery stick, roughly chopped
- 1 bouquet garni
- 2 leeks, sliced
- 50g/2oz butter
- 2 tbsp plain flour
- grated zest 1 lemon
- bunch parsley, chopped
- 3 tbsp crème fraîche
- 250g/9oz ready-made puff pastry
- little beaten egg, to glaze

1 Heat the slow cooker if necessary. Put the chicken, carrot, onion, celery and bouquet garni in the pot with enough boiling water almost to cover. Cover and cook on High for 5–6 hours until the chicken is cooked through.

2 Lift the chicken on to a plate. Strain the stock, discarding the veggies, and measure out and reserve 500ml/18fl oz.

3 Heat oven to 200C/180C fan/gas 6. Strip the meat from the chicken and put it into a pie dish.

4 Fry the leeks in butter until soft. Stir in the flour, then gradually add the reserved stock, cooking until the sauce is smooth. Add the zest, parsley, crème fraîche and some seasoning. Pour over the chicken.

5 Roll out the pastry and trim to 5cm/2in larger than the dish. Brush the edges of the dish with water and lay on the pastry, tucking the edges under to make a double layer around the rim. Press the pastry edges to seal. Brush with the egg and bake for 30–35 minutes.

· ·

PER SERVING (6) 401 kcals, protein 28g, carbs 21g, fat 23g, sat fat 10g, fibre 1g, sugar 2g, salt 0.60g

Tender duck & pineapple red curry

This slow-cooked curry improves if made up to 2 days ahead, without the pineapple. Then simply add the pineapple and reheat.

 9 hours   6   Easily halved

- 6 duck legs
- 2 tbsp light soft brown sugar, plus extra to taste (optional)
- 4 tbsp Thai red curry paste
- 400ml can coconut milk
- 2 tbsp Thai fish sauce, plus extra to taste (optional)
- 6 kaffir lime leaves
- 1 small pineapple, peeled, cored and cut into chunks
- 1 red chilli, deseeded and finely sliced (optional)
- a few Thai basil leaves (optional)
- jasmine rice, to serve

1 Heat the slow cooker if necessary. Dry-fry the duck legs in an ovenproof frying pan or casserole dish on a low heat for a good 10–15 minutes, turning once, until coloured all over. Put in the slow-cooker pot. Add the sugar, curry paste, coconut milk, fish sauce and lime leaves. Cover and cook for 8 hours on Low until the duck is really tender.

2 Lift the duck legs into a serving dish and skim any fat from the sauce, if you like. Stir in the pineapple, and half the chilli and the Thai basil leaves, if using. Cover and heat through for a few minutes, then add more fish sauce for salt, or sugar for sweetness. Garnish with the remaining chilli, if using, and serve with jasmine rice.

PER SERVING 659 kcals, protein 38g, carbs 20g, fat 49g, sat fat 20g, fibre 2g, sugar 18g, salt 2.29g

Chicken & red-wine casserole with herby dumplings

If this sauce tastes too strongly of wine for you, then before you add it to the slow-cooker pot boil it in a pan to burn off the alcohol kick.

 6½ hours 6

- 3 tbsp olive oil
- 6 boneless chicken breasts
- 300g/10oz large flat mushrooms
- 3 tbsp plain flour
- 3 onions, each peeled and cut into 8 wedges
- 200g/8oz smoked bacon lardons
- 3 garlic cloves, peeled and sliced
- 2 tbsp redcurrant sauce
- 300ml/½ pint each red wine and chicken stock

FOR THE DUMPLINGS
- 100g/4oz each self-raising flour and fresh white breadcrumbs
- 1 tbsp wholegrain mustard
- 140g/5oz butter, cubed
- 2 tsp thyme leaves, plus extra to garnish
- 2 tbsp chopped parsley
- 2 medium eggs

1 Heat the slow cooker if necessary. Halve the chicken breasts. Heat the oil in a frying pan and, in batches, brown the chicken. Slice the mushrooms and transfer to the slow-cooker pot with the flour, onions, lardons, garlic, redcurrant sauce, red wine and stock, and season. Cover and cook on High for 4 hours.

2 After 3½ hours of cooking, make the dumplings. Put the flour, breadcrumbs, mustard and butter in a food processor, and whizz to crumbs. Beat the eggs then add the thyme, parsley, and some seasoning, and work together to make a moist dough. Using floured hands, roll the mixture into six balls.

3 Remove the lid after 4 hours and sit the dumplings on top of the casserole. Cover and cook for 1–2 hours until the chicken is tender and the dumplings have puffed up. Serve scattered with the extra thyme leaves.

PER SERVING 701 kcals, protein 47g, carbs 38g, fat 37g, sat fat 17g, fibre 3g, sugar 1g, salt 2.55g

Chicken & cider fricassee

. . . .

Chicken cooked with tarragon and cider makes a quintessentially British, crowd-pleasing casserole.

 7 hours   8

- 2 tbsp olive oil
- 2 whole chickens, each jointed into 8 pieces, or 16 bone-in chicken pieces
- 300g/10oz smoked streaky bacon, chopped
- 2 onions, finely chopped
- 2 carrots, finely chopped
- 2 celery stalks, finely chopped
- 500g pack chestnut mushrooms, quartered
- 4 tbsp plain flour
- 500ml bottle dry cider
- 750ml/1¼ pints chicken stock
- 5 thyme sprigs
- few parsley stalks
- 2 bay leaves
- 150ml pot double cream
- 2 tbsp English mustard
- small pack tarragon leaves, chopped
- seasonal veg, to serve

1 Heat the slow cooker if necessary. Heat the o in a large deep pan. Season the chicken and brown in batches. Transfer to a plate. Reduce the heat and add the bacon to the pan. Fry until golden and crisp, then set aside with the chicken. Add the onions, carrots and celery to the pan, scraping up any brown bits with a wooden spoon. Fry over a low heat until soft and starting to brown.

2 Add the mushrooms and continue to cook for a further 4–5 minutes. Stir in the flour until it disappears, then stir in the cider and stock, and bring to the boil, scraping any bits stuck to the bottom of the pan.

3 Tie the thyme sprigs, parsley stalks and bay leaves together with kitchen string. Put the chicken and bacon, vegetables, liquid and tied herbs in the slow cooker. Cover and cook on Low for 6 hours until the chicken is tender and coming away from the bone.

4 Add the cream, mustard and tarragon to the sauce and season to taste. Serve with seasonal vegetables.

. . . .

PER SERVING 657 kcals, protein 50g, carbs 15g, fat 41g, sat fat 15g, fibre 3g, sugar 6g, salt 2.2g

French duck confit

In this recipe, duck legs are cooked French-style in goose fat, making them incredibly tender. The dish can be made up to a month ahead and kept in the fridge.

🕐 2 days   2

- 25g/1oz sea salt flakes
- 2 tsp crushed black peppercorns
- 4 fresh bay leaves
- 2 large or 4 small duck legs (about 550g/1lb 4oz total)
- 1 tsp thyme leaves, plus 2–4 sprigs
- 340g can goose or duck fat, melted
- 300ml/½ pint groundnut oil (optional)

1 At least 24 hours before serving, mix together the salt, pepper and bay leaves. Add the duck legs and rub in the salt. Cover and leave in the fridge.
2 Next day, heat the slow cooker if necessary. Wipe the salt from the duck and put the legs in a single layer in the slow-cooker pot. Add the thyme, plus the bay and peppercorns from the salt mix and pour over the melted fat. If it doesn't cover the duck, top up with groundnut oil. Cover and cook on Low for 10–12 hours. The duck skin should be creamy.
3 Transfer the legs to a bowl and strain in the fat, pushing the duck under until fully submerged. (This can now be kept in the fridge for up to 1 month.)
4 Heat oven to 220C/200C fan/gas 7. Remove the duck legs from the fat, wiping off any excess. Season and sit the legs on a wire rack in a roasting tin. Cook for 30 minutes until the skin is crisp (for a really crispy skin, flash under a hot grill for a few minutes at the end).

PER SERVING 529 kcals, protein 43g, carbs 1g, fat 38g, sat fat 12g, fibre none, sugar none, salt 1.37g

Hot game pies

Serve these at a dinner party and you'll wow your guests. Just serve with some green veg or cabbage, plus mash, if you like.

 7 hours 8

- 4 tbsp olive oil
- 800g/1lb 12oz mixed diced game (such as pheasant, rabbit and venison)
- 3 venison sausages
- 100g/4oz pancetta, skinned and cut into small cubes, or use bacon lardons
- 200ml/7fl oz red wine
- 140g/5oz mixed mushrooms
- 400g/14oz shallots, peeled
- 200g/8oz parsnips, peeled and chopped
- 1 tbsp tomato purée
- thyme and rosemary sprigs and 2 bay leaves, plus extra to garnish (optional)
- 700ml/1¼ pints beef or game stock
- 375g sheet puff pastry, thawed if frozen
- 1 egg, beaten

1 Heat the slow cooker if necessary. Heat some of the oil in a large frying pan and brown the meat, sausages and pancetta in batches – add more oil for each batch. Transfer to the slow-cooker pot. Pour the wine into the frying pan and boil for 1 minute. Tip into the slow cooker with the vegetables, purée, herbs and stock.

2 Cover and cook on High for 5–6 hours until really tender, then remove the meat and veg with a slotted spoon and divide among eight small pie dishes. Pour the liquid into a pan and boil until reduced to about 500ml/18fl oz. Divide among the dishes.

3 Heat oven to 220C/200C fan/gas 7. Roll out the pastry and cut out eight rounds big enough to fit on to the dishes. Brush the dish edges with egg and stick on pastry tops, pressing to seal. Top with pastry cut-outs and garnish with herbs, if you like, then brush with more egg. Bake for 20–25 minutes until risen and golden.

PER SERVING 987 kcals, protein 62g, carbs 39g, fat 61g, sat fat 23g, fibre 10g, sugar 2g, salt 3.14g

Chicken cassoulet

. . . .

This cheat's cassoulet will become such a favourite you'll want to make it every week; so it's lucky it's so easy!

 7 hours 6

- 2 tbsp olive oil
- 250g/9oz packs lardons or cubetti di pancetta
- 1 large onion, sliced
- 6 Toulouse or chunky Italian sausages
- 6 boneless skinless chicken thighs
- 3–4 large garlic cloves, chopped
- 2 bay leaves
- 1 tsp dried thyme
- 3 x 400g cans butter beans, drained and rinsed
- 300ml/½ pint chicken stock
- 2 tbsp tomato purée
- 400g can chopped tomatoes
- 85g/3oz coarse white breadcrumbs

1 Heat the slow cooker if necessary. Heat 1 tablespoon of the oil in a non-stick frying pan and fry the lardons or pancetta, onion and sausages until the onion has softened a bit and the sausages are golden. Tip into the slow-cooker pot, then top with the chicken thighs, garlic, bay and thyme. Tip the beans on top, followed by the stock, tomato purée and chopped tomatoes.

2 Cover and cook on High for 5–6 hours until the chicken is tender.

3 If your slow-cooker pot can go under the grill give everything in the pot a good stir, season and scatter with the breadcrumbs. Or tip everything into a casserole or ovenproof dish then season and scatter with the breadcrumbs. Grill until crispy.

. . . .

PER SERVING 879 kcals, protein 60g, carbs 36g, fat 56g, sat fat 18g, fibre 7g, sugar none, salt 6g

Hot & sticky ribs

Ribs are best cooked slowly and gently, until the meat is almost falling off the bone – then made sticky just at the last minute

 6-8 hours 6  Easily halved

- 1.25kg/2lb 12oz pork ribs
- 3 tbsp soy sauce
- 3 tbsp rice vinegar
- 1 tsp Chinese five-spice powder

FOR THE GLAZE

- 3 tbsp sweet chilli sauce
- 1 tbsp dark soy sauce
- 1 tbsp plum jam
- 1 tbsp ground ginger
- 1 large garlic clove, crushed
- good pinch dried chilli flakes

1 Heat the slow cooker if necessary. Put the ribs in the slow cooker and pour over the soy and vinegar, sprinkle on the five-spice and pour on enough water just to cover. Cook on High for 5–7 hours, until really tender.

2 Heat grill to high. Mix together all the glaze ingredients to make a thick sauce. When the ribs are tender, remove them from the pot with a slotted spoon and pat dry with some kitchen paper. Transfer to a roasting tin. Brush on the glaze and grill for 5–15 minutes, turning, until sticky. Pile on to a platter and serve.

PER SERVING 218 kcals, protein 19g, carbs 5g, fat 14g, sat fat 5g, fibre none, sugar 4g, salt 1.20g

Sticky spiced-lamb shanks

These aromatic lamb shanks are a real treat for two. Serve with fragrant rice or couscous, or some lovely warm flatbreads.

 10-11 hours 2  Easily doubled

- 1½ tbsp olive oil
- 2 lamb shanks
- 3 onions, sliced
- 4 garlic cloves, sliced
- ½ cinnamon stick
- 1 tbsp each cumin and coriander seeds, crushed
- pinch chilli flakes
- 400g can chopped tomatoes
- 500ml/18fl oz chicken or vegetable stock
- 2 tbsp pomegranate molasses
- 4 dried apricots, chopped
- 4 dried figs, chopped
- handful coriander, chopped

1 Heat the slow cooker if necessary. Heat the oil in a pan and brown the shanks for a couple of minutes, turning them as you go. Put in the slow-cooker pot with all the remaining ingredients except the coriander. Cover and cook on Low for 9–10 hours until the lamb is really tender.

2 Remove the shanks from the pot and wrap in foil to keep warm. Tip the contents of the pot into a pan and boil down the juices until thick and saucy. Season, then serve the shanks scattered with coriander.

PER SERVING 1,114 kcals, protein 95g, carbs 64g, fat 55g, sat fat 23g, fibre 10g, sugar 52g, salt 1.93g

Chilli con carne

· ·

This is an ideal dish for entertaining families, and any leftovers freeze really well; so if you've got a big slow cooker it's definitely worth making a double batch.

🕐 10½ hours   🥘 4–6   ◑ Easily halved or doubled

- 2 tbsp olive oil
- 2 large onions, halved and sliced
- 3 large garlic cloves, chopped
- 2 tbsp mild chilli powder
- 2 tsp each ground cumin and dried oregano
- 1kg pack lean minced beef
- 400g can chopped tomatoes
- 2 large red peppers, deseeded and cut into chunks
- 10 sun-dried tomatoes, halved
- 3 x 400g cans red kidney beans, drained and rinsed
- 2 beef stock cubes
- avocado, salad, rice or tortilla chips and some soured cream, to serve

1 Heat the slow cooker if necessary. Heat the oil in a large pan, and fry the onions for 8 minutes. Add the garlic, spices and oregano, and cook for 1 minute, then gradually add the mince, stirring well until browned. Tip into the slow-cooker pot and stir in the chopped tomatoes, peppers, sun-dried tomatoes and beans, then crumble in the stock cubes and season to taste.

2 Cover and cook on Low for 8–10 hours. Serve with avocado or a big salad with avocado in it, some rice or tortilla chips and a bowl of soured cream.

· ·

PER SERVING (4) 820 kcals, protein 75g, carbs 58g, fat 34g, sat fat 12g, fibre 16g, sugar 21g, salt 5g

Lancashire hotpot

Everybody loves Lancashire hotpot, and it's even easier to make when you've got a slow cooker.

 5-6 hours  4

- 5 tbsp lard or olive oil
- 900g/2lb stewing lamb, cut into large chunks
- 2 medium onions, chopped
- 4 carrots, peeled and sliced
- 50g/2oz plain flour
- 2 tsp Worcestershire sauce
- 300ml/½ pint lamb or chicken stock
- 2 bay leaves
- 2 thyme sprigs
- 900g/2lb potatoes, peeled and sliced

1 Heat the slow cooker if necessary. Heat 3 tablespoons of the lard or oil in a large frying pan and brown the lamb in batches, removing to a plate.

2 Fry the onions and carrots in the pan with 1 tablespoon more of the lard or oil until golden. Stir in the flour and allow to cook for a couple of minutes. Tip into the slow-cooker pot with the lamb, Worcestershire sauce, stock, bay, thyme and some seasoning. Give everything a good stir, then push down evenly in the pot. Arrange the sliced potatoes on top of the meat, then dot with the remaining lard or drizzle with the rest of the oil. Sprinkle over a little more seasoning, cover, and cook on High for 4–5 hours until the lamb and potatoes are tender.

3 If you like, finish the dish under a hot grill for 5–8 minutes until the potatoes are browned and crisp.

PER SERVING 891 kcals, protein 59g, carbs 60g, fat 48g, sat fat 23g, fibre 6g, sugar 11g, salt 0.93g

Big-batch Bolognese

Don't worry if your slow cooker is too small for this recipe, it is really easy to reduce the quantities, and it will taste delicious no matter how much you make.

 8–10 hours 12  Easily halved

- 4 tbsp olive oil
- 6 rashers smoked bacon, chopped
- 1.5kg/3lb 5oz lean minced beef
- 4 onions, finely chopped
- 3 carrots, finely chopped
- 4 celery sticks, finely chopped
- 500g/1lb 2oz mushrooms, sliced
- 8 garlic cloves, crushed
- 2 tbsp dried mixed herbs
- 2 bay leaves
- 4 x 400g cans chopped tomatoes
- 6 tbsp tomato purée
- large glass red wine (optional)
- 4 tbsp red wine vinegar
- 1 tbsp sugar
- Parmesan shavings, to garnish
- cooked pasta, to serve

1 Heat the slow cooker if necessary. Heat the o in a very large pan and fry the bacon and mince, in batches, until browned. Tip into the slow-cooker pot, and stir in the vegetables, garlic, herbs, chopped tomatoes, purée, wine, if using, vinegar and sugar with some seasoning.

2 Cover and cook on Low for 6–8 hours, then uncover, turn to High and cook for another hour until thick and saucy, and the mince is tender. Serve scattered with shavings of Parmesan and some pasta.

PER SERVING 321 kcals, protein 31g, carbs 8g, fat 19g, sat fat 7g, fibre 2g, sugar 7g, salt 0.7g

Minted lamb & pea stew

This light, summery stew is brilliant eaten at any time of the year – just add some crusty bread to mop up the juices in the bowl.

 7–9 hours 4

- 1 tbsp sunflower oil
- 350g/12oz lean lamb leg, cubed
- 4 shallots, quartered
- 2 leeks, sliced
- 4 carrots, thickly sliced
- 400g/14oz potatoes, cut into large cubes
- 3 tbsp plain flour, seasoned
- 500ml/18fl oz lamb or chicken stock
- 300g/10oz frozen peas, defrosted
- handful mint leaves, to garnish

1 Heat the slow cooker if necessary. Heat the oil in a large pan, then brown the lamb in batches over a high heat for 2 minutes each time. Layer the shallots, leeks, carrots and potatoes in the slow-cooker pot. Top with the lamb, scatter over the flour and pour over the stock. Cover and cook on Low for 6–8 hours until the lamb is tender.

2 Stir in the peas, re-cover, but turn off the slow cooker and leave for 15 minutes to heat through. Season and scatter with mint to serve.

PER SERVING 357 kcals, protein 28g, carbs 37g, fat 12g, sat fat 4g, fibre 10g, sugar 11g, salt 1.38g

Slow-roast pork rolls

This is perfect food for friends – little work in preparation but packed full of flavour after long, slow cooking.

 5-6 hours 4

- 1.25kg/2lb 12oz pork shoulder joint, scored and tied
- 2 tsp thyme leaves
- 1 tsp fennel seeds
- 1 tbsp olive oil
- buttered soft bread rolls and apple chutney, or sauce, to serve

1 Heat the slow cooker if necessary. If the pork skin isn't already scored for you, score it with a small, sharp knife. Mix together the thyme, fennel seeds, oil and 1 teaspoon salt with a good grinding of black pepper. Rub this over the top and ends of the pork. Brown the pork in a large pan, turning frequently, until well browned, or roast at 220C/200C fan/gas 7 for 30 minutes until browned.

2 Transfer the pork to the slow-cooker pot and cook on High for 4–5 hours until the meat can be shredded with a spoon. Remove the fat and use a couple of forks to shred the pork from the joint. Sandwich in soft buttered rolls with apple chutney or sauce, warmed or at room temperature.

PER SERVING 408 kcals, protein 61g, carbs trace, fat 18g, sat fat 7g, fibre none, sugar none, salt 0.39g

Cottage pie

This makes enough to feed an army, but it freezes really well and can also be halved very easily if you have a small slow cooker.

 7–9 hours   10   Easily halved

- 3 tbsp olive oil
- 1.25kg/2lb 12oz minced beef
- 2 onions, finely chopped
- 3 carrots, chopped
- 3 celery sticks, chopped
- 3 tbsp plain flour
- 1 tbsp tomato purée
- large glass red wine (optional)
- 500ml/18fl oz beef stock
- 4 tbsp Worcestershire sauce
- few thyme sprigs
- 2 bay leaves

FOR THE MASH
- 1.8kg/4lb potatoes, chopped
- 225ml/8fl oz milk
- 25g/1oz butter
- 200g/8oz strong Cheddar, grated

1 Heat the slow cooker if necessary. Heat the oil in a large pan and fry the mince until browned in batches. Tip into the slow-cooker pot and stir in the vegetables, flour, purée, wine (if using), stock, Worcestershire sauce and herbs with some seasoning. Cover and cook on High for 4–5 hours.

2 When the beef and veg has about 30 minutes to go, make the mash. Boil the potatoes until tender, then mash with the milk, butter, and three-quarters of the cheese. Season.

3 Spoon the lamb mixture into an ovenproof dish or dishes. Pipe or spoon on the mash, then sprinkle over the remaining cheese. Grill until golden and ready to serve.

PER SERVING 600 kcals, protein 37g, carbs 40g, fat 34g, sat fat 16g, fibre 4g, sugar 7g, salt 1.15g

Sausage & bean one-pot

This sausage stew is delicious with or without the crumbs, but they do add a nice crunch to the finished dish.

 7-9 hours   4  Easily doubled

- 1 tbsp olive oil
- 8 pork sausages
- 2 leeks, trimmed then thinly sliced
- 1 carrot, roughly chopped
- 1 tbsp chopped sage leaves, plus a little extra for the crumbs
- 1 garlic clove, crushed
- 200ml/7fl oz beef stock
- 400g can chopped tomatoes
- 2 x 400g cans cannellini beans, drained and rinsed
- 2 slices day-old white or brown bread, whizzed into breadcrumbs

1 Heat the slow cooker if necessary. Heat the oil in a large pan, add the sausages and brown for a few minutes. Remove from the pan and put in the slow-cooker pot with the leeks and carrot, sage, garlic, stock, tomatoes and beans. Season, cover and cook on Low for 6–8 hours.

2 When the sausages are done, mix the breadcrumbs with a little more chopped sage. Heat grill to medium. If your slow-cooker pot can go under the grill, scatter the crumbs over, or tip everything into an ovenproof dish and scatter over the crumbs. Grill until golden and ready to serve – about 5 minutes.

PER SERVING 605 kcals, protein 39g, carbs 40g, fat 34g, sat fat 12g, fibre 11g, sugar 10g, salt 3.45g

Slow-cooked Irish stew

Middle neck or scrag-end of lamb are flavoursome cuts and perfect for braising. This traditional casserole contains filling pearl barley, too.

 8 hours 6

- 1 tbsp sunflower oil
- 200g/8oz smoked streaky bacon, preferably in one piece, skinned and cut into chunks
- 900g/1lb 15oz cheap stewing lamb, such as middle neck or scrag-end (ask at your butcher counter), cut into large chunks
- small bunch thyme
- 3 onions, thickly sliced
- 5 carrots, cut into big chunks
- 6 medium potatoes, cut into big chunks
- 700ml/1¼ pints lamb stock
- 3 bay leaves
- 85g/3oz pearl barley
- 1 large leek, washed and cut into chunks
- small knob butter

1. Heat the slow cooker if necessary, then heat the oil in a frying pan. Sizzle the bacon until crisp, tip into the slow-cooker pot, then brown the chunks of lamb in the pan in batches. Transfer to the slow-cooker pot along with the thyme, onions, carrots, potatoes, stock, bay leaves and enough water to cover the lamb. Cover and cook on Low for 6–7 hours.
2. Stir in the pearl barley and leek, and cook on High for 1 hour more until the pearl barley is tender.
3. Stir in the butter, season and serve scooped straight from the dish.

PER SERVING 673 kcals, protein 40g, carbs 40g, fat 39g, sat fat 16g, fibre 7g, sugar 11g, salt 1.4g

Braised pork with plums

Pork shoulder is the perfect cut of meat for the slow cooker as it really needs long, slow braising to become lovely and tender.

 10 hours, plus marinating 8

- about 1.6kg/3lb 8oz pork shoulder, cut into very large chunks
- 5 tbsp each rice wine and soy sauce
- generous thumb-sized knob ginger
- 5 garlic cloves
- 1 red chilli, deseeded and finely chopped
- 2 tbsp vegetable oil
- bunch spring onions, finely sliced
- 1 cinnamon stick
- 2 star anise
- 2 tsp Chinese five-spice powder
- 2 tbsp each sugar (any type) and tomato purée
- 500ml/18fl oz chicken stock
- 6 ripe plums, halved and stoned

1 Mix the pork with the rice wine and soy, plus half of the ginger, garlic and chilli. Marinate for 1–24 hours.

2 Heat the slow cooker if necessary. Heat the oil in a large pan. Tip in half the spring onions, the remaining ginger, garlic and chilli, and the cinnamon, star anise, five-spice, sugar and purée. Fry until soft, then lift the pork from the marinade and add to the pan, frying until the meat is sealed but not browned. Tip everything into the slow-cooker pot with the marinade and stock. Cover and cook for 8–9 hours on Low.

3 Skim any fat off the surface halfway through cooking, if you can. Stir in the plums an hour before the end of the cooking time.

4 Scoop the meat and plums from the pot. Tip the rest of the slow-cooker contents into a large pan and boil for 5–10 minutes until the sauce is slightly syrupy. Return the pork and plums to warm through gently, then scatter with the remaining spring onions to serve.

PER SERVING 530 kcals, protein 40g, carbs 11g, fat 36g, sat fat 13g, fibre 1g, sugar 10g, salt 2.87g

Slow-cooked shoulder of lamb

Simplicity itself – cooking lamb shoulder slowly means the meat will melt away from the bone.

 9½ hours  4

- 2 garlic cloves, finely chopped
- 1 tbsp roughly chopped oregano leaves
- 3 tbsp olive oil
- 1 shoulder of lamb, boned and tied (about 1.5kg/3lb 5oz)
- 400g/14oz pearl onions or shallots
- 1 tbsp gravy browning or Marmite
- 250ml/9fl oz lamb stock
- 100g/4oz fresh peas
- 100g/4oz fresh broad beans
- 2 Little Gem lettuce, cut into quarters
- juice 1 lemon
- small handful mint or coriander leaves, roughly chopped, plus extra leaves to garnish

1 Heat the slow cooker if necessary. Mix the garlic, oregano and olive oil with some salt and black pepper. Slash the lamb all over and rub the mixture into the meat. Heat a large frying pan or casserole and brown the lamb, turning, for 15 minutes or so until browned.

2 Lift the lamb into the slow-cooker pot. Add the pearl onions or shallots and browning or Marmite, and pour over the stock. Cover and cook on Medium for 8 hours until the lamb is really tender.

3 Stir in the peas and broad beans, cover and cook for another 30 minutes.

4 Lift out the lamb and cover in foil to rest. Stir the lettuce, lemon juice and herbs into the veg with some seasoning. Turn off the slow cooker, but cover and leave for 5 minutes to heat through. Return the lamb to serve or transfer everything to a serving dish. Garnish with some mint or coriander and serve.

PER SERVING 976 kcals, protein 72g, carbs 9g, fat 73g, sat fat 35g, fibre 5g, sugar 5g, salt 0.95g

Spiced shepherd's pie

· · · · · · · · · · · · · · · · · · · ·

This shepherd's pie has a Moroccan twist that should liven up supper a bit – and, unbelievably, it only uses five ingredients.

 7–9 hours   4

- 4 tbsp olive oil
- 500g pack minced lamb
- 3 tbsp Moroccan spice mix
- 400g can chopped tomatoes with garlic and onion
- 750g/1lb 10oz cooked potatoes

1 Heat the slow cooker if necessary. Heat 1 tablespoon of the olive oil in a large non-stick frying pan, then fry the lamb, stirring well, and half the spice mix until browned. Tip into the slow-cooker pot with the tomatoes, then season, cover, and cook on Low for 6–8 hours.

2 Crush the potatoes with the remaining oil and spice mix. Heat grill to high and tip the mince mixture into an ovenproof dish. Scatter with the potatoes and grill for 8 minutes until the potatoes are crispy and golden.

· ·

PER SERVING 562 kcals, protein 29g, carbs 41g, fat 33g, sat fat 11g, fibre 3g, sugar 3g, salt 3.62g

Beef stew with horseradish dumplings

This is easy, delicious and dead simple. Use a cut with real flavour, like shin or neck, and let it cook slow and long. Serve it with lightly buttered peas.

 10–13 hours 8

- 2kg/4lb 8oz beef shin, neck or stewing steak, chopped into large chunks
- 100g/4oz plain flour
- 25g/1oz dripping, lard or oil
- 500g/1lb 2oz shallots, peeled
- 1 litre/1¾ pints beef stock

FOR THE DUMPLINGS
- 140g/5oz suet
- 350g/12oz self-raising flour
- 50g/2oz fresh grated horseradish
- fresh or frozen peas, to serve

1 Heat the slow cooker if necessary. Put the beef into a large bowl or bag and toss in the flour. Heat the dripping, lard or oil in a large pan and brown the beef in batches, then add to the slow cooker with the shallots and stock. Cook on Low for 8–9 hours, until really tender.

2 When the beef has got about 30 minutes to go, make the dumplings. Mix the suet, flour and horseradish together, and season. Gradually add 1–2 tablespoons water to the dry ingredients until you have a firmish dough (you might need a bit more water). Shape into 12 dumplings. Put on to the stew and cover again, turn to High and cook for 1–2 hours more until the dumplings are puffed up and cooked through. Serve with some buttery peas.

PER SERVING 752 kcals, protein 64g, carbs 48g, fat 35g, sat fat 15g, fibre 3g, sugar 3g, salt 1.16g

Sweet & sour pork stir-fry

This traditionally quick-cooked Chinese favourite is also delicious slow cooked, and better still this version is low in fat.

 1½ hours 2  Easily doubled

- 227g can pineapple slices in juice, drained and chopped, juice reserved
- 1 tbsp cornflour
- 1 tbsp tomato sauce
- 1 tsp each soy sauce and brown sugar
- 2½ tbsp rice wine vinegar or white wine vinegar
- 1 tbsp sunflower oil
- 200g/8oz stir-fry pork strips, trimmed of fat
- 1 red pepper, deseeded and cut into chunks
- 3 spring onions, quartered and shredded
- rice or noodles, to serve

1 Heat the slow cooker if necessary. Mix 4 tablespoons of the reserved pineapple juice gradually into the cornflour until smooth, then stir in the tomato sauce, soy, sugar, vinegar and oil.

2 Mix the sauce with the pork, pepper, pineapple chunks and most of the spring onions in the slow-cooker pot. Cover and cook on High for 1 hour until the pork is tender. Scatter with the remaining spring onions and serve with rice or noodles.

PER SERVING 284 kcals, protein 24g, carbs 31g, fat 8g, sat fat 2g, fibre 2g, sugar 24g, salt 0.96g

Hearty lamb stew

· ·

A delicious nourishing casserole that's easily adapted to suit your tastes: vary the herbs, swap the stock for a can of chopped tomatoes, or use lentils instead of beans.

 6–7 hours 4  Easily doubled

- 1 tbsp vegetable oil
- 500g pack cubed stewing lamb
- 1 onion, thickly sliced
- 2 carrots, thickly sliced
- 2 leeks, thickly sliced
- 400ml/14fl oz hot chicken or vegetable stock
- 1 tsp dried rosemary or 1 sprig
- 400g can cannellini beans, drained and rinsed
- crusty bread or boiled potatoes, to serve (optional)

1 Heat the slow cooker if necessary. Heat the o[il] in a large pan, tip in the lamb and brown for a few minutes, in batches if necessary.

2 Tip the lamb into the slow-cooker pot and stir in the onion, carrots and leeks. Pour over the stock, and add the herbs and beans. Cover and cook for 5–6 hours on High until the lamb is tender. Serve with some crusty bread or potatoes, if you like.

· ·

PER SERVING 397 kcals, protein 38g, carbs 19g, fat 20g, sat fat 8g, fibre 6g, sugar 8g, salt 1.15g

Spaghetti & meatballs

Everybody's favourite. By using some sausages you get maximum flavour into the meatballs without needing lots of herbs or flavourings.

 6½ hours 10 Easily halved

- 8 good-quality pork sausages, skinned
- 1kg/2lb 4oz minced beef
- 1 onion, finely chopped
- ½ x large bunch flat-leaf parsley, finely chopped
- 85g/3oz Parmesan, grated, plus extra to taste
- 100g/4oz fresh breadcrumbs
- 2 eggs, beaten with a fork
- olive oil, for frying
- few basil leaves, to garnish
- cooked spaghetti and Parmesan, to serve

FOR THE SAUCE
- 3 tbsp olive oil
- 4 garlic cloves, crushed
- 4 x 400g cans chopped tomatoes, 2 cans drained
- 125ml/4fl oz red wine (optional)
- 3 tbsp caster sugar
- ½ x large bunch flat-leaf parsley, finely chopped

1 Heat the slow cooker if necessary. For the meatballs, mix the sausage meat, mince, onion, parsley, Parmesan, crumbs, eggs and some seasoning. Roll into about 50 golf-ball-sized meatballs, then brown in the oil, in batches, in a non-stick frying pan.

2 For the sauce, mix the oil, garlic, tomatoes, wine (if using), sugar, parsley and some seasoning in the slow-cooker pot. Drop in the meatballs, cover and cook on High for 4–5 hours. If the sauce is thin, cook uncovered for the last hour. Eat with spaghetti, an extra grating of Parmesan and a scattering of basil.

PER SERVING 870 kcals, protein 46g, carbs 95g, fat 37g, sat fat 13g, fibre 5g, sugar 13g, salt 1.34g

Turkish lamb pilaf

This is a complete meal in one, with no need for any extra accompaniments, so spoon straight from the pot and tuck in!

 4½ hours 4

- 1 tbsp olive oil
- 2 cinnamon sticks, broken in half
- 1 tsp each ground cumin, coriander and turmeric
- 1 large onion, halved and sliced
- 500g/1lb 2oz lean lamb neck fillet, cubed
- 250g/9oz basmati rice
- 1 lamb or vegetable stock cube
- 12 ready-to-eat-dried apricots
- small handful toasted pine nuts or toasted flaked almonds
- handful mint leaves, roughly chopped

1 Heat the slow cooker if necessary, then heat the oil in a frying pan. Fry the cinnamon, spices and onion together for 5–10 minutes until starting to turn golden. Turn up the heat, stir in the lamb, and fry until the meat changes colour. Tip into the slow-cooker pot with the rice and stir to mix.

2 Pour in 500ml/18fl oz boiling water, crumble in the stock cube, add the apricots, then season to taste. Cook on Low for 3–4 hours until the rice is tender and the stock has been absorbed. Toss in the pine nuts or almonds and the mint, and serve.

PER SERVING 584 kcals, protein 32g, carbs 65g, fat 24g, sat fat 9g, fibre 3g, sugar none, salt 1.4g

Lamb & spinach curry

If you're going out to work and want to put the curry on in the morning before you leave, simply swap the lamb steak for stewing lamb and cook on Low for the day.

 2½ hours 4 Easily doubled

- ½ tsp cumin seeds
- 2 tsp sunflower oil
- 200g/8oz lean lamb steak, cubed
- 1 red pepper, deseeded and sliced
- 1 green chilli, deseeded and sliced
- 2 tbsp curry paste
- 225g can chopped tomatoes, drained
- 160ml can coconut cream
- 100g bag baby leaf spinach
- ½ x 20g pack coriander, chopped
- rice or naan bread, to serve

1 Heat the slow cooker if necessary. Dry-fry the cumin seeds for about 20 seconds in a pan, then add the oil and stir-fry the lamb for about 1 minute until browned, but not cooked all the way through. Tip into the slow-cooker pot with the peppers, chilli, curry paste, tomatoes and coconut cream. Cover and cook on High for 1½–2 hours until the lamb is tender.

2 Stir in the spinach and coriander with some seasoning if it needs it. Serve with rice or naan bread.

PER SERVING 205 kcals, protein 13g, carbs 6g, fat 15g, sat fat 8g, fibre 2g, sugar 5g, salt 0.66g

Courgette, sausage & rigatoni bakes

This thrifty and comforting pasta bake for two is made with a punchy garlic and chilli-spiked tomato sauce, then topped with mozzarella.

 1 hour 2

- 1 tbsp olive oil
- 4 good-quality pork sausages
- 2 courgettes, sliced on the diagonal then chopped into batons
- 3 garlic cloves, finely sliced
- pinch chilli flakes
- 400g can chopped tomatoes
- 200g/8oz rigatoni
- ½ x 150g ball mozzarella, patted dry and torn into chunks

1 Heat the slow cooker. Heat the oil in a large frying pan. Squeeze the sausage meat out of the skins, breaking it into little chunks, and pop in the pan. Fry for 8 minutes until golden and cooked through, then scoop into the slow-cooker pot. Add the courgettes, garlic, chilli flakes, tomatoes, pasta and 250ml/9fl oz water to the slow-cooker pot, season and cook on High for 30 minutes, until the pasta is al dente.

2 Spoon the pasta and sauce into two small flameproof dishes. Heat the grill to high. Dot the cheese on top of the sausage dishes, then put under the grill until the cheese is golden and bubbling (about 5–10 minutes), and serve.

PER BAKE 834 kcals, protein 38g, carbs 73g, fat 44g, sat fat 16g, fibre 5g, sugar 13g, salt 3.1g

Goulash in a dash

• •

If you like your goulash with a bit of kick, use hot paprika, but if you're feeding kids you'll probably want to stick to sweet paprika.

 10½ hours   4   Easily halved or doubled

- 1 tbsp vegetable oil
- 400g/14oz lean stewing beef, diced into large chunks
- 1 tbsp paprika
- 500g/1lb 2oz new potatoes, halved
- 2 red peppers, deseeded and cut into chunks
- 600ml/1 pint hot beef stock
- 600ml/1 pint passata with onion and garlic
- handful parsley leaves, roughly chopped
- natural yogurt or soured cream, to garnish

1 Heat the slow cooker if necessary. Heat the oil in a large non-stick pan and fry the beef to brown. If your pan is small, fry in two batches. Tip the meat into the slow-cooker pot.

2 Sprinkle the paprika over the beef, then tip in potatoes, peppers, stock and passata. Give it all a good stir, cover and cook on Low for 8–10 hours until the beef and potatoes are tender. Stir in the parsley and serve with a dollop of yogurt or soured cream.

• •
PER SERVING 319 kcals, protein 30g, carbs 35g, fat 8g, sat fat 2g, fibre 3g, sugar 11g, salt 1.3g

Prawn, pea & tomato curry

. . . .

This has to be the healthiest curry ever: high in fibre, low in fat, it also provides three of your 5-a-day.

 4½ hours  4

- 1 tbsp vegetable oil
- large knob ginger, peeled and chopped
- 6 garlic cloves, roughly chopped
- 3 tbsp curry paste (we used Patak's tikka masala paste)
- 6 ripe tomatoes, each cut into 8 wedges
- 2 onions, halved, each cut into 6 wedges
- 400g/14oz raw peeled king prawns
- 250g/9oz frozen peas
- small bunch coriander, leaves chopped, to garnish
- basmati rice or chapattis, to serve

1 Heat the slow cooker if necessary. Whizz the oil, ginger, garlic, curry paste and all but eight of the tomato wedges to a paste. Scrape into the slow-cooker pot and stir in the onion wedges. Cover and cook on High for 3 hours until the onions are tender.
2 Mix in the remaining tomato wedges, the prawns and peas. Cover and cook for 30 minutes–1 hour, until the prawns are cooked through. Scatter with coriander, then serve with rice or chapattis.

. . . .

PER SERVING 236 kcals, protein 24g, carbs 18g, fat 8g, sat fat 1g, fibre 6g, sugar 10g, salt 1.24g

Crab-stuffed tomatoes

∙∙∙∙∙∙∙∙∙∙∙∙∙∙∙∙∙∙∙∙∙∙

Use a variety of tomatoes if you like, big and small – especially if you're entertaining – as it'll look really interesting when you come to serve.

 2½ hours 4-5

- a little olive oil for greasing and drizzling
- 10 mixed-variety big tomatoes
- 140g/5oz crab meat, a mixture of brown and white (or just white, if you prefer)
- 4 tbsp white breadcrumbs
- 3 tbsp grated Parmesan
- 50g/2oz butter, melted
- 2 tbsp double cream
- 2 tsp Dijon mustard
- 1 tsp Worcestershire sauce
- few pinches cayenne pepper
- small bunch chives, finely snipped

1 Heat the slow cooker if necessary and oil the base of the pot. Neatly slice the top off each tomato and keep it, then scoop out the flesh with a teaspoon and reserve 4 tablespoons of this, too. Season the tomato insides with salt and black pepper.

2 Make the filling. Scoop the crab meat into a bowl. Set aside 1 tablespoon each of the breadcrumbs and Parmesan, and mix the rest into the crab meat with the melted butter and all the remaining ingredients except about half of the snipped chives. Season and stuff into each tomato.

3 Top each tomato with the reserved breadcrumbs and Parmesan mixed with about half of the remaining chives. Sit in the pot, season and drizzle with a little oil. Bake for 1–2 hours on High until the tomatoes are just cooked but not falling apart, popping the lids on halfway. Before serving, scatter over the remaining chives.

∙∙∙∙∙∙∙∙∙∙∙∙∙∙∙∙∙∙∙∙∙∙∙∙∙∙∙

PER SERVING (4) 310 kcals, protein 12g, carbs 17g, fat 22g, sat fat 11g, fibre 2g, sugar 8g, salt 1.15g

Linguine with tuna sauce

A simple tuna-and-tomato pasta sauce can be really delicious if done well, and this one is packed with flavour.

 3½ hours 4

- 4 tbsp extra virgin olive oil
- 3 tbsp chopped flat-leaf parsley
- 2 garlic cloves, finely chopped
- 1 red chilli, deseeded and finely chopped
- 1cm/½in knob ginger, peeled and finely chopped
- 450g/1lb passata
- about 400g/14oz tuna in olive oil, from jar or can, drained and flaked
- 375g/13oz linguine

1 Heat the slow cooker if necessary. Put the oil, 2 tablespoons of the parsley, the garlic, chilli, ginger and passata into the slow-cooker pot. Cover and cook on High for 2–3 hours.

2 Stir in the tuna, re-cover and cook on High for another 30 minutes.

3 Cook the linguine according to the pack instructions then drain well. Toss the linguine into the tuna sauce and sprinkle over the remaining parsley. Divide among four bowls and serve immediately.

Easy prawn pilaf

Rinse the rice thoroughly as the more starch you can get rid of, the better the finished dish will be.

🕐 4⅛ hours   🍴 4

- 300g/10oz easy-cook basmati rice
- 2 tbsp korma curry paste
- 1 small onion, finely chopped
- 700ml/1¼ pints chicken or vegetable stock
- 150g pack cooked peeled prawns, defrosted if frozen
- 140g/5oz frozen peas
- 1 red chilli, deseeded and sliced
- handful coriander leaves, to scatter
- lemon wedges, to garnish

1 Heat the slow cooker if necessary. Rinse the rice in a sieve until the water runs clear. Heat a large wide pan and dry-fry the curry paste with the onions for 4–5 minutes until the onions begin to soften. Scrape the onions into the slow-cooker pot with the rice and stir to coat the rice in the curry paste. Add the stock, cover and cook on High for 2–3 hours, until the rice is tender.

2 Stir in the prawns, peas and chilli. Cover again and cook for another 30 minutes on Low.

3 Fluff up the rice grains with a fork and season if you want. Scatter over the coriander and serve with lemon wedges to squeeze over.

PER SERVING 340 kcals, protein 18g, carbs 65g, fat 3g, sat fat 1g, fibre 2g, sugar none, salt 2.38g

Creamy spiced mussels

· ·

If you have never bought fresh mussels before, you'll find they are surprisingly quick and easy to prepare.

 2 hours 4

- 2 shallots, finely chopped
- 25g/1oz butter
- 1 tsp plain flour
- 1–2 tsp curry paste
- 150ml/¼ pint dry white wine
- 2kg/4lb 8oz fresh mussels
- 100ml/3½fl oz crème fraîche
- chopped parsley, to garnish
- chips or bread, to serve

1 Heat the slow cooker if necessary. Put the shallots, butter, flour, curry paste and wine into the slow-cooker pot. Cover and cook on High for 1 hour.

2 Scrub the mussels in a large bowl of cold water and discard any that are open. Tip into the slow-cooker pot, re-cover and cook on High for 1½ hours until just about all the mussels are open and cooked. Discard any that haven't opened during cooking.

3 Stir the crème fraîche into the sauce, warming it through. Scoop out the mussels into four bowls and pour over the sauce. Scatter with parsley and serve with chips or bread to mop up the juices.

· ·

PER SERVING 285 kcals, protein 19g, carbs 6g, fat 18g, sat fat 10g, fibre 1g, sugar none, salt 1.27g

Seafood pasta

· ·

This all-in-one dish is completely cooked in your slow cooker so it'll be one of the easiest suppers you'll ever make.

 9 hours 4

- 1 tbsp olive oil
- 1 onion, chopped
- 1 garlic clove, chopped
- 1 tsp paprika
- 400g can chopped tomatoes
- 700ml/1¼ pints chicken stock (from a cube is fine)
- 300g/10oz spaghetti, roughly broken
- 240g pack frozen mixed seafood, defrosted
- handful parsley leaves, chopped, and lemon wedges, to garnish

1 Heat the slow cooker if necessary. Mix the oil, onion, garlic, paprika, tomatoes and stock in the slow-cooker pot. Cover and cook on Low for 7–8 hours.
2 Turn the slow cooker to High and stir in the spaghetti and seafood. Cover and cook for another 30 minutes–1 hour until the spaghetti is cooked.
3 Season to taste, sprinkle with the parsley and serve with lemon wedges to squeeze over.

· ·
PER SERVING 370 kcals, protein 23g, carbs 62g, fat 5g, sat fat 1g, fibre 4g, sugar none, salt 1.4g

Red Thai salmon curry

You can easily experiment with this curry to suit your mood. Swap the Thai red curry paste for green or yellow, and the salmon for white fish or prawns.

 2½ hours 4

- 1 tsp vegetable or sunflower oil
- 1 tbsp Thai red curry paste
- 1 onion, sliced
- 250ml/9fl oz reduced-fat coconut milk
- 2 x 250g skinless salmon fillets, cut into chunks
- 200g/8oz trimmed green beans
- plain rice, to serve

1 Heat the slow cooker if necessary. Warm the oil in a large pan, then add the curry paste. Stir in the onion, then cook gently for about 5 minutes until softened.

2 Transfer the onion to the slow-cooker pot with the coconut milk, salmon chunks and beans. Cook on Low for 1½–2 hours until the fish flakes easily and the beans are cooked but have a little crunch. Serve with plain rice.

PER SERVING 326 kcals, protein 27g, carbs 5g, fat 22g, sat fat 9g, fibre 2g, sugar 4g, salt 0.46g

Creamy smoked haddock & saffron kedgeree

. . . .

Use good-quality undyed fish in this creamy brunch rice dish with hard-boiled eggs and saffron.

 2 hours 40 minutes   4

- 300g/10oz basmati rice
- 50g/2oz butter
- 3 eggs
- 100ml/3½fl oz white wine
- 600ml/1 pint hot vegetable or fish stock
- 1 tsp cayenne pepper
- pinch saffron threads
- 1 tbsp mild curry powder
- a little freshly grated nutmeg
- 200ml/7fl oz double cream
- 500g/1lb 2oz naturally smoked haddock fillet, skin removed
- small handful flat-leaf parsley, chopped
- 1 lemon, cut into wedges, to garnish

1 Heat the slow cooker if necessary. Put the rice, butter, eggs (in their shells), wine, stock and spices into the slow-cooker pot and cook on High for 2 hours.

2 Fish the eggs out of the pan and set aside. Stir the cream into the rice, put the haddock on top, cover and cook for a further 30 minutes.

3 Peel the eggs and roughly chop. Stir through the rice with the parsley and serve with lemon wedges on the side.

. . . .

PER SERVING 424 kcals, protein 22g, carbs 17g, fat 30g, sat fat 16g, fibre 1g, sugar 2g, salt 2.15g

Sea bass with black-bean sauce

This dish is perfect for a special meal for two, as it's really impressive but actually dead easy to make.

 1½ hours 2

- 1 sea bass, head on, gutted
- 2cm/¾in knob ginger, peeled and thinly sliced
- 2 tbsp Shaohsing rice wine
- 100ml/3½fl oz black bean sauce
- 2 spring onions, shredded
- small handful coriander, leaves only
- jasmine rice, to serve

1 Wash the fish in cold running water, pat dry with kitchen paper, then slash three or four slits into the skin on both sides. Season all over with salt and ground white pepper. Put ginger slices in the slits of the fish and inside the cavity. Put the fish on an upturned plate that fits inside your slow cooker. Turn the cooker to High and add the rice wine. Cover and cook on High for an hour without taking off the lid.

2 While the fish is cooking, heat the black bean sauce according to the pack instructions and stir in 2 tablespoons water to thin it a little.

3 Carefully remove the fish. Drizzle with the sauce, and scatter with the spring onions and coriander leaves. Serve with jasmine rice.

PER SERVING 511 kcals, protein 49g, carbs 11g, fat 29g, sat fat 5g, fibre 1g, sugar 8g, salt 7.67g

Spaghetti alle vongole

Clams are easy to cook with – they just need a little preparation first.

 1¾–2¼ hours   2   Easily doubled

- 500g/1lb 2oz fresh clams in shells
- 2 ripe tomatoes, chopped
- 2 tbsp olive oil
- 1 fat garlic clove, chopped
- 1 small or ½ large red chilli, finely chopped
- splash white wine (about ½ small glass)
- 140g/5oz spaghetti
- 2 tbsp chopped flat-leaf parsley
- bread, to serve

1 Heat the slow cooker if necessary. Rinse the clams in several changes of cold water. Discard any that are open or damaged. Add the clams to the slow-cooker pot with the chopped tomatoes, olive oil, garlic, chilli and white wine. Cook on High for 1½–2 hours, until the clams are open.

2 About 30 minutes before the clams are ready, cook the spaghetti according to the pack instructions. Drain the pasta, then tip the pasta into the slow cooker with the parsley and toss together. Serve in bowls with bread for mopping up the juices.

PER SERVING 409 kcals, protein 16g, carbs 56g, fat 13g, sat fat 2g, fibre 3g, sugar 5g, salt 0.10g

Chorizo, new potato & haddock one-pot

This is a great simple way to cook fish, as you get a fantastic result with minimum effort. If you don't have any sherry in the cupboard, white wine will do.

 3–4 hours   2

- 50g/2oz chorizo, peeled and thinly sliced
- 450g/1lb salad or new potatoes, sliced
- 4 tbsp dry sherry
- 2 thick skinless white fish fillets (try sustainably caught haddock)
- good handful cherry tomatoes, halved
- 20g bunch parsley, chopped
- extra virgin olive oil, for drizzling
- crusty bread, to serve

1 Heat the slow cooker if necessary then add the chorizo and potatoes to the slow-cooker pot, tossing them well with 3 tablespoons of the sherry. Cover and cook on High for 2–3 hours until the potatoes are just tender. Move them around the pot a bit after 1 hour.

2 Season the fish well. Give the potatoes another stir, add the cherry tomatoes and most of the chopped parsley, then lay the fish on top. Splash over the remaining sherry, put the lid on again, then leave to cook for 30 minutes, or until the fish has turned white and flakes easily when prodded. Scatter the whole dish with the remaining parsley and drizzle with the extra virgin olive oil. Serve straight away with crusty bread.

PER SERVING 534 kcals, protein 47g, carbs 39g, fat 19g, sat fat 4g, fibre 3g, sugar 5g, salt 0.79g

Leek & mackerel penne bake

This is a superfast, filling meal for busy midweek winter nights. Great made with smoked haddock, too.

 2½ hours 2

- 2 leeks, trimmed, washed and sliced
- knob butter
- 700ml/1¼ pints vegetable stock
- 200ml pot reduced-fat crème fraîche
- 1 tbsp capers
- 175g/6oz penne
- 2 small smoked mackerel fillets, skinned and flesh flaked into large chunks
- 25g/1oz breadcrumbs

1 Heat the slow cooker if necessary. Add the leeks and the butter to the slow-cooker pot and cook on High for 1 hour, until soft.

2 Mix the stock and crème fraîche, then tip into the leeks with the capers and pasta, and cook on High for about an hour until the pasta is tender.

3 Heat grill to high. Tip the creamy veg and pasta into an ovenproof dish and gently stir in the fish. Scatter with the crumbs and grill until golden and crisp.

PER SERVING 925 kcals, protein 35g, carbs 84g, fat 52g, sat fat 20g, fibre 5g, sugar 8g, salt 2.72g

Easy paella

This is a cheat's version of the Spanish favourite. Serve with crusty bread and a glass of something cold.

 3 hours   4

- 1 tbsp olive oil
- 1 onion, chopped
- 1 tsp each hot smoked paprika and dried thyme
- 300g/10oz paella or risotto rice, rinsed until the water runs clear
- 3 tbsp dry sherry or white wine (optional)
- 400g can chopped tomatoes with garlic
- 900ml/1½ pints chicken stock
- 400g bag frozen mixed seafood
- juice ½ lemon, other ½ cut into wedges, to garnish
- handful flat-leaf parsley, roughly chopped, to scatter
- crusty bread, to serve

1 Heat the slow cooker if necessary. Heat the oil in a large frying pan. Add the onion and soften for 5 minutes. Stir in the paprika, thyme and rice, stir for 1 minute, then splash in the sherry or wine, if using. Once the sherry or wine has evaporated, scrape everything into the slow-cooker pot. Stir in the tomatoes and stock. Season, cover and cook on High for about 2 hours.

2 Stir the frozen seafood into the pot, cover and cook for another 30 minutes or until the prawns are cooked through and the rice is tender. Squeeze over the lemon juice, scatter with parsley and serve with the extra lemon wedges and some crusty bread.

PER SERVING 431 kcals, protein 34g, carbs 66g, fat 5g, sat fat 1g, fibre 3g, sugar 5g, salt 2.14g

Rich paprika seafood bowl

This easy seafood stew makes a nice lunch or light supper with a big chunk of crusty bread to mop up the sauce.

 9–11 hours 4

- large bunch flat-leaf parsley, leaves and stalks separated
- 1 tbsp olive oil
- 2 onions, halved and thinly sliced
- 2 celery sticks, finely chopped
- 2–3 tsp paprika
- 200g/8oz roasted red peppers, thickly sliced
- 400g can chopped tomatoes with garlic
- few fresh mussels (optional)
- 400g/14oz skinless white fish fillet, cut into very large chunks
- crusty bread, to serve

1 Heat the slow cooker if necessary. Put the parsley stalks, half the leaves, the oil and some seasoning into a food processor, and whizz to a paste. Add the paste and the onions, celery, paprika, peppers and chopped tomatoes to the slow-cooker pot. Give everything a good stir, then cover and cook on Low for 8–10 hours.

2 If using the mussels, nestle these into the sauce and scatter the fish on top. Re-cover, then cook on High for 30 minutes–1 hour until the fish is just flaking and the mussels have opened – discard any that stay shut. Gently stir the seafood into the sauce, season, then serve in bowls with a scattering of the remaining parsley leaves and some slices of crusty bread.

PER SERVING 192 kcals, protein 22g, carbs 12g, fat 7g, sat fat 1g, fibre 4g, sugar 8g, salt 1.14g

Macaroni cheese

. . . .

This is a really clever recipe that needs no fiddly white sauce and still results in a creamy version of this family classic.

 1 hour 4

- 25g/1oz cornflour
- 700ml/1¼ pints semi-skimmed milk
- 200ml/7fl oz crème fraîche
- 1 heaped tsp English mustard powder
- 1 large garlic clove, finely chopped
- 1 bay leaf
- generous pinch crushed dried chillies
- a little freshly grated nutmeg
- 250g/9oz macaroni
- 140g/5oz extra mature Cheddar, grated
- 50g/2oz fresh breadcrumbs
- 50g/2oz Parmesan, grated
- 450g/1lb mix of tomatoes, such as cherry and medium vine
- bunch spring onions, ends trimmed

1 Heat the slow cooker if necessary. Mix the cornflour to a paste with a splash of the milk in a big pan, then gradually stir in the rest of the milk, followed by the crème fraîche, mustard powder, garlic, bay, chillies and nutmeg. Bring to the boil then turn off and leave to infuse for 5 minutes.

2 Strain the sauce into the slow-cooker pot and stir in the macaroni and Cheddar. Cover and cook on High for 30 minutes or until the pasta is cooked.

3 Heat grill to high. Pour the cheesy pasta into an ovenproof dish and scatter over the breadcrumbs, Parmesan, tomatoes and spring onions. Grill until crisp and golden.

. . . .

PER SERVING 789 kcals, protein 31g, carbs 77g, fat 42g, sat fat 25g, fibre 4g, sugar 16g, salt 1.40g

Five-a-day tagine

This tagine not only provides all of your 5-a-day, but it's high in fibre, low in fat and a good source of iron, folic acid and vitamin C too!

 7-9 hours 4 Easily halved or doubled

- 4 carrots, cut into chunks
- 4 small parsnips or 3 large, cut into chunks
- 3 red onions, cut into wedges
- 2 red peppers, deseeded and cut into chunks
- 2 tbsp olive oil
- 1 tsp each ground cumin, paprika, cinnamon and mild chilli powder
- 400g can chopped tomatoes
- 2 small handfuls soft dried apricots
- 2 tsp honey
- couscous or jacket potatoes, to serve

1 Heat the slow cooker if necessary. Mix the veg, oil, spices, chopped tomatoes, apricots and honey in the slow-cooker pot. Cover and cook on Low for 6–8 hours until all the veg is tender.
2 Stir in some seasoning and serve with couscous or jacket potatoes.

PER SERVING 272 kcals, protein 7g, carbs 45g, fat 8g, sat fat 1g, fibre 12g, sugar 32g, salt 0.35g

Indian butternut squash curry

This is a fantastic curry for vegetarians, or serve it as a side dish alongside some other curries for a big group of friends.

 7–9 hours 4 Easily doubled

- 1 tbsp olive oil
- 1 red onion, diced
- 2 tbsp mild curry paste
- 1 butternut squash, peeled, deseeded and diced
- 4 large tomatoes, roughly chopped
- 400g can chickpeas, drained and rinsed
- 150ml/¼ pint vegetable stock
- 3 tbsp fat-free Greek yogurt
- small handful coriander, chopped
- brown basmati rice and chapattis, to serve

1 Heat the slow cooker if necessary. Mix the oil, onion and curry paste in the slow cooker pot, throw in the squash and give it a good stir, then add the tomatoes, chickpeas and stock. Cover and cook on Low for 6–8 hours until the squash is tender.
2 Turn off the heat and stir through the yogurt and coriander. Serve with basmati rice and some chapattis, if you like.

Black-bean chilli

This vegetarian chilli can bubble happily away while you're out for the day, then when you get home you can enjoy a low-fat supper containing all your 5-a-day.

 9 hours   4–6   Easily halved or doubled

- 2 tbsp olive oil
- 4 garlic cloves, finely chopped
- 2 large onions, chopped
- 3 tbsp sweet paprika or mild chilli powder
- 3 tbsp ground cumin
- 3 tbsp cider vinegar
- 2 tbsp brown sugar
- 2 x 400g cans chopped tomatoes
- 2 x 400g cans black beans, drained and rinsed
- rice, to serve, plus a few, or one, of the following – crumbled feta, chopped spring onions, sliced radishes, avocado chunks, soured cream

1 Heat the slow cooker if necessary. Heat the olive oil in a frying pan, and fry the garlic and onions for 5 minutes until almost softened.

2 Add the paprika or chilli and the cumin, cook for a few minutes, then scrape into the slow-cooker pot with the vinegar, sugar, tomatoes, beans and some seasoning. Cover and cook on Low for 8 hours. Serve with rice and the accompaniments of your choice in small bowls.

PER SERVING (4) 339 kcals, protein 17g, carbs 50g, fat 10g, sat fat 1g, fibre 8g, sugar 20g, salt 1.45g

Spicy spaghetti with garlic mushrooms

A spicy pasta supper, perfect for vegetarians or just for a tasty, healthy dinner.

 8 hours 4 Easily doubled

- 2 tbsp olive oil
- 1 garlic clove, thinly sliced
- 1 onion, finely chopped
- 1 celery stick, finely chopped
- 400g can chopped tomatoes
- ½ red chilli, deseeded and finely chopped (or use dried chilli flakes)
- 250g pack chestnut mushrooms, thickly sliced
- 300g/10oz spaghetti
- small bunch parsley, leaves only, to garnish

1 Heat the slow cooker if necessary. Mix all the ingredients except for the pasta and parsley in the slow-cooker pot. Cover and cook on Low for 6–7 hours.
2 Just before you're ready to eat, cook the spaghetti in a large pan according to the pack instructions. Drain well, tip back into the pan and stir in the mushroom sauce. Scatter with parsley and serve.

PER SERVING 346 kcals, protein 12g, carbs 62g, fat 7g, sat fat 1g, fibre 5g, sugar 7g, salt 0.35g

Golden veggie shepherd's pie

. . . .

Dried lentils are cheap and nutritious; we've used green here, but red work just as well. Never add salt to lentils while they are cooking, though – it toughens their skins.

 7 hours   10  Easily halved

- 50g/2oz butter
- 2 onions, chopped
- 4 carrots, diced
- 1 celery head, chopped
- 4 garlic cloves, finely chopped
- 200g pack chestnut mushrooms, sliced
- 2 bay leaves
- 1 tbsp dried thyme
- 500g pack dried green lentils
- 100ml/3½fl oz red wine (optional)
- 1.7 litres/3 pints vegetable stock
- 3 tbsp tomato purée
- 2kg/4lb 8oz mashed potato
- 50g/2oz Cheddar, grated

1 Heat the slow cooker if necessary. Heat the butter in a pan, then gently fry the onions, carrots, celery and garlic for 15 minutes until soft and golden. Tip into the slow-cooker pot and stir in the mushrooms, herbs and lentils. Pour over the wine, if using, and stock, cover and cook on High for 5–6 hours – do not season with salt at this stage.

2 Now season to taste; then turn off the slow cooker and stir in the tomato purée. Divide the lentil mixture among one, two or individual ovenproof dishes, then top with the mash and scatter over the cheese. If the mash is cold, bake the dish in a hot oven for 30 minutes until piping hot, or if using hot mash just put under a hot grill until golden and starting to crisp.

. . . .
PER SERVING 449 kcals, protein 19g, carbs 68g, fat 13g, sat fat 7g, fibre 10g, sugar 9g, salt 0.59g

Mumbai potato wraps with minted yogurt relish

This low-fat potato curry is fantastic in these Indian-style wraps, but you can just as easily spoon it over rice, or serve it in bowls with a wedge of naan bread to dunk in.

 4 hours 4  Easily halved

- 1 onion, sliced
- 2 tbsp medium curry powder
- 400g can chopped tomatoes
- 750g/1lb 10oz potatoes, diced
- 2 tbsp mango chutney, plus extra to taste (optional)
- 100g/4oz low-fat natural yogurt
- 1 tsp mint sauce from a jar
- 8 plain chapattis
- small bunch coriander, to garnish

1 Heat the slow cooker if necessary. Tip the onion, curry powder, chopped tomatoes, potatoes and mango chutney into the slow-cooker pot with 50ml/2fl oz boiling water. Stir everything together, then cover and cook for 3 hours on High until the potatoes are tender. Season well.

2 When the potato curry is almost ready, mix together the yogurt and mint sauce, and warm the chapattis according to the pack instructions.

3 To serve, spoon some of the potatoes on to a chapatti and top with a few sprigs of coriander. Drizzle with the minted-yogurt relish, adding extra mango chutney, if you wish, then roll up and eat.

PER SERVING 426 kcals, protein 14g, carbs 83g, fat 7g, sat fat 1g, fibre 6g, sugar 12g, salt 1.22g

Summer vegetables & chickpeas

Tomato-based stews like this are perfect for slow cookers and ideal for making ahead – vary the vegetables depending on what's in your fridge or in season.

 7-9 hours 4  Easily halved

- 3 courgettes, thickly sliced
- 1 aubergine, cut into chunks
- 3 garlic cloves, chopped
- 2 red peppers, deseeded and chopped into chunks
- 2 large baking potatoes, peeled and cut into bite-sized chunks
- 1 onion, chopped
- 1 tbsp coriander seeds
- 4 tbsp olive oil
- 400g can chopped tomatoes
- 400g can chickpeas, drained and rinsed
- small bunch coriander, roughly chopped
- crusty bread, to serve

1 Heat the slow cooker if necessary. Tip all of the vegetables into the slow-cooker pot and toss with the coriander seeds, most of the olive oil and some salt and black pepper. Pour over the tomatoes and chickpeas, then cover and cook on Low for 6–8 hours until the potatoes are tender.

2 Season to taste, drizzle with the remaining olive oil, then scatter over the coriander. Serve from the pot or pile into a serving dish. Eat with hunks of crusty bread.

PER SERVING 327 kcals, protein 11g, carbs 40g, fat 15g, sat fat 2g, fibre 9g, sugar 13g, salt 0.51g

Cauliflower cheese & spinach pasta bakes

. . . .

Somewhere between macaroni cheese and cauliflower cheese, these pasta bakes are perfect for a cold day when only a really satisfying supper will do.

 2½ hours   6   Easily halved

- 50g/2oz melted butter, plus 1 tbsp
- 50g/2oz plain flour
- 700ml/1¼ pints milk, plus extra splash (optional)
- 1 tsp Dijon mustard
- 100g/4oz extra mature Cheddar, grated
- 25–50g/1–2oz blue cheese
- ½ tsp finely grated nutmeg
- 1kg/2lb 4oz cauliflower (2 medium ones), cut into florets
- 250g/9oz penne
- 4 handfuls spinach leaves
- 300g/10oz tomato pasta sauce
- 25g/1oz toasted pine nuts
- green salad or garlic bread, to serve

1 Heat the slow cooker if necessary. Stir together the butter and flour in the slow-cooker pot, then gradually whisk in the milk and mustard. Stir in most of the Cheddar, half of the blue cheese, the nutmeg and the cauliflower with some seasoning. Cover and cook on High for 1 hour until the cauliflower is almost tender. Add the pasta, mixing well so that it is covered by the sauce (add a splash more milk, if you need to), and cook for a further 30 minutes–1 hour until the pasta is cooked.

2 Heat grill to high. Stir through the spinach to wilt, then spoon half into an ovenproof dish or six individual dishes. Dollop the tomato sauce over the top, then spoon the rest of the cauliflower–pasta mixture over the tomato sauce. Scatter with the remaining cheeses and the pine nuts, and grill on high until golden and bubbling. Good served with green salad or garlic bread.

. . . .

PER BAKE 515 kcals, protein 23g, carbs 54g, fat 25g, sat fat 12g, fibre 6g, sugar 15g, salt 1.28g

Creamy veggie korma

This veggie curry is high in fibre and a really good source of iron if you're feeding vegetarians.

🕐 5 hours   4

- 1 tbsp vegetable oil
- 1 onion, finely chopped
- 3 cardamom pods, bashed
- 2 tsp each ground cumin and coriander
- ½ tsp ground turmeric
- 1 green chilli
- thumb-sized knob ginger
- 1 garlic clove, crushed
- 800g/1lb 12oz mixed vegetables, such as carrots, cauliflower, potato and courgette, chopped
- 400ml/14fl oz hot vegetable stock
- 200g/8oz frozen peas, defrosted
- 200g/8oz natural yogurt
- 2 tbsp ground almonds
- chopped toasted flaked almonds and a few coriander leaves, to garnish
- basmati rice or naan bread, to serve

1 Heat the slow cooker if necessary. Heat the oil in a large pan. Cook the onion with the dry spices over a low heat for 5–6 minutes until the onion is light golden. Deseed and finely chop the chilli, peel and finely chop the ginger then add to the pan with the garlic. Cook for 1 minute, then tip into the slow-cooker pot.

2 Throw the mixed vegetables into the pot, add the stock, cover and cook on Low for 4 hours until the potatoes are tender.

3 Stir in the peas, yogurt and ground almonds with some seasoning. Stand for 5 minutes to heat through, then scatter with a few flaked almonds and coriander leaves, and serve with basmati rice or some naan bread.

PER SERVING 257 kcals, protein 10g, carbs 31g, fat 11g, sat fat 5g, fibre 7g, sugar 16g, salt 0.42g

Sweet potato & spinach bake

If you want to make this dish healthier, swap the double cream for single, or use half-fat crème fraîche. It will look a little split and grainy, but it will still taste great.

 3 hours 4

- 300ml/½ pint double cream
- 1 garlic clove, peeled
- 2 thyme or rosemary sprigs
- 250g bag frozen leaf spinach
- freshly grated nutmeg
- butter, for greasing
- 850g/1lb 14oz sweet potatoes, peeled and thinly sliced (about 3mm/⅛in thick)
- 25g/1oz grated hard cheese, such as Cheddar, Parmesan or a veggie alternative

1 Heat the slow cooker, if necessary. Put the cream, garlic and herb sprigs into a small pan and slowly bring to just below boiling. Turn off the heat, season and leave to infuse.

2 Put the spinach into a colander, pour over a kettle of boiling water and leave to drain for a few minutes. Then squeeze out as much water as possible. Season with some salt, black pepper and the freshly grated nutmeg.

3 Grease the pot of the slow cooker generously with butter and spread half the sweet potato slices across the bottom. Top with a layer of spinach, then the remaining potato. Pour over the cream mixture through a sieve, to remove the garlic and herbs, then sprinkle with the cheese. Cover and bake for 2 hours on High until tender. If you like, remove the pot and put under a high grill to crisp up the top.

PER SERVING 611 kcals, protein 7g, carbs 48g, fat 45g, sat fat 25g, fibre 7g, sugar 14g, salt 0.61g

Creamy celery gratin

This dish works equally well with fish, chicken or pork, or if you were to add a green salad and a chunk of bread it would make a great vegetarian main course.

 2½ hours 6

- 2 celery heads, trimmed
- 50g/2oz butter, melted
- 1 onion, thinly sliced
- 2 bay leaves
- 100g/4oz breadcrumbs
- 50g/2oz walnuts, roughly chopped
- 75ml/2½fl oz white wine
- 250ml/9fl oz vegetable or chicken stock
- 100ml/3½fl oz double cream
- 25g/1oz grated Parmesan

1 Heat the slow cooker if necessary. Cut any thick celery sticks in half and trim all of it into thumb-sized lengths. Mix in the slow-cooker pot with half the butter, the onion and bay. Cover and cook on High for 2 hours until tender.

2 When the celery is almost cooked, mix the remaining butter with the crumbs and walnuts in a small bowl.

3 Heat grill to medium. When the celery is tender, tip it into a heatproof dish and stir in the white wine, stock and double cream with some seasoning. Scatter with the breadcrumb mix and the Parmesan. Grill for 2–3 minutes, until the sauce bubbles and breadcrumbs are crisp. Let it sit for 5 minutes before serving.

PER SERVING 304 kcals, protein 7g, carbs 17g, fat 24g, sat fat 11g, fibre 2g, sugar 3g, salt 0.91g

Cabbage with beans & carrots

This all-in-one side dish is clever and delicious, and also versatile enough to be served with a variety of different things.

 3¼ hours 6

- 25g/1oz butter
- 4 rashers smoked streaky bacon, chopped
- 2 carrots, peeled and chopped into small chunks
- 1 Savoy cabbage, quartered, cored and shredded
- 400g can haricot beans, drained and rinsed
- 300ml/½ pint chicken stock

1 Heat the slow cooker if necessary. Melt the butter in a pan and fry the bacon until it starts to crisp. Tip the bacon into the slow-cooker pot with the carrots, cabbage, beans and stock. Cover and cook on High for 2–3 hours until the carrots are tender.
2 Season and serve.

PER SERVING 169 kcals, protein 10g, carbs 15g, fat 8g, sat fat 3g, fibre 7g, sugar 8g, salt 1.17g

Tomatoes stuffed with pesto rice

Stuffed with spinach, pesto rice and melting mozzarella, these tomatoes make a tasty veggie supper.

 2 hours 3

- 1 tbsp olive oil, plus extra for drizzling
- 6 large beef tomatoes
- 100g/4oz basmati rice
- 3 tbsp pesto
- 100g/4oz grated mozzarella
- 80g bag spinach leaves, roughly chopped
- 400ml/14fl oz hot stock

1 Heat the slow cooker and oil the base of the pot. Slice the tops off the tomatoes and set aside. Scoop out the insides with a teaspoon, keeping the tomatoes intact. Discard the tomato seeds, but roughly chop the tomato tops. Tip the rice into a bowl, mix with the pesto and season well. Mix in the chopped tomato, three-quarters of the mozzarella, the spinach and some seasoning.

2 Spoon the rice mixture into the tomatoes and pack the stuffed tomatoes tightly into the slow-cooker pot. Pour the stock over and around the tomatoes, filling the pot with as much liquid as possible. Drizzle with a little more olive oil and cook for 1–2 hours, until the tomatoes are tender and the rice is cooked. Scoop the tomatoes into a baking dish, scatter with the remaining cheese and put under a high grill until melted and golden.

PER SERVING 377 kcals, protein 13g, carbs 36g, fat 18g, sat fat 6g, fibre 6g, sugar 11g, salt 1.3g

Braised lettuce & peas

. . . .

If you have a double slow cooker, cook this alongside one of our stews, but if you only have a single pot make this up to step 2 the day before, then finish in a pan to serve.

 2½ hours   6    Easily doubled

- 16 shallots or pearl onions, halved and peeled
- 200ml/7fl oz vegetable or chicken stock
- 300g/10oz peas
- 3 Baby Gem lettuces

1 Heat the slow cooker if necessary. Add the shallots or onions and the stock to the slow-cooker pot, cover and cook for 2 hours on High until tender.
2 Stir in the peas and cook for 15–20 minutes more until tender.
3 Turn off the heat, finely shred the lettuce and stir into the slow cooker. Leave for 2 minutes to wilt, then serve.

. . . .
PER SERVING 73 kcals, protein 3g, carbs 6g, fat 4g, sat fat 1g, fibre 3g, sugar 2g, salt 0.01g

Sticky spiced red cabbage

. . . .

This delicious cabbage is a great addition to a Sunday roast. It can be made up to 2 days ahead and reheated with a splash of water.

🕐 7–9 hours   🥧 6–8   🌓 Easily halved

- 1 tbsp olive oil
- 1 medium-sized red cabbage, quartered, cored and shredded
- finger-sized knob ginger, peeled and finely chopped
- 2 onions, sliced
- 1 tsp ground allspice
- 1 tbsp mustard seeds
- 100g/4oz golden caster sugar
- 150ml/¼ pint red wine vinegar

1 Heat the slow cooker if necessary. Mix all the ingredients in the slow-cooker pot, then cove and cook on Low for 6–8 hours until the cabbage is tender, stirring halfway through the cooking time, if you can.
2 Tip the cabbage into a large bowl and serve.

PER SERVING (6) 137 kcals, protein 3g, carbs 27g, fat 3g, sat fat none, fibre 4g, sugar 24g, salt 0.04g

Sweet braised onions

· ·

This vegetarian side dish works well with a Sunday lunch. The whole onions are sweetened with balsamic vinegar and maple syrup.

 4 hours   6

- olive oil, for greasing and drizzling
- 12 small red onions
- 1½ tbsp balsamic vinegar
- 2 tbsp maple syrup

1 Heat the slow cooker, if necessary. Cut about 1cm/½in off the top and bottom of each onion and peel off the skin. Nestle the onions in the pot so that they fit snugly together in a single layer. Drizzle over a little more oil, the balsamic vinegar, maple syrup and 3 tablespoons water; season. Cover the onions loosely with baking parchment and cook for 3–4 hours until tender.

· ·
PER SERVING 89 kcals, protein 2g, carbs 14g, fat 3g, sat fat none, fibre 2g, sugar 11g, salt 0.1g

Hot chocolate mousses

· ·

These are not as rich as most chocolate pots, so the whole family should love them. If you fancy, just cook the whole thing in the slow-cooker pot and let everyone dive in.

 2 hours   3–4   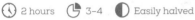 Easily halved

- 2 x 58g Mars bars, chopped into pieces
- 50ml/2fl oz milk
- 100g bar dark chocolate
- 3 egg whites
- chocolate shavings, to decorate

1 Heat the slow cooker if necessary. Check you have three or four heatproof pots, cups or mugs that will fit in your slow cooker pot.

2 Put the Mars bars, milk and chocolate in a heavy-based pan. Cook over a very gentle heat, stirring constantly, until the chocolate has melted. Transfer to a bowl and leave to cool for 15 minutes. Whisk frequently with a wire whisk to blend in any pieces of fudge that rise to the surface to leave it smooth.

3 Whisk the egg whites in a separate bowl until softly peaking. Using a metal spoon, fold a quarter of the whites into the chocolate sauce to lighten it, then fold in the remainder.

4 Divide the mixture among the heatproof pots. Cover the top of each with a dome of foil and sit in the slow-cooker pot. Pour in enough boiling water to come halfway up the sides of the mousse pots, cover, and cook for 1 hour on High until softly set. Serve topped with chocolate shavings.

· ·

PER SERVING 369 kcals, protein 8g, carbs 50g, fat 17g, sat fat 9g, fibre 1g, sugar 39g, salt 0.60g

Banana rice pudding with cinnamon sugar

This delicious rice pudding is low in fat but still beautifully creamy.

 3⅛ hours 4

- 175g/6oz pudding rice
- 2 tbsp custard powder
- 850ml/1½ pints skimmed milk
- 4 tbsp demerara sugar
- 2 large bananas, thinly sliced
- ½ tsp ground cinnamon

1 Heat the slow cooker if necessary. Rinse the rice in a sieve until the water runs clear. Put the custard powder, milk, half the sugar and the rice into the slow-cooker pot, and stir. Cover and cook on High for 2–3 hours until the rice is tender and creamy.

2 Stir in the bananas – take care as the rice will be very hot. Mix the remaining sugar and the cinnamon together in a small bowl. Spoon the creamy banana rice into bowls and serve sprinkled with the crunchy cinnamon sugar.

PER SERVING 347 kcals, protein 11g, carbs 78g, fat 1g, sat fat none, fibre 1g, sugar 37g, salt 0.29g

Peach fool

· · · · · · · · · · · · · · · · · · · ·

Intensely fruity, lightly spiced peaches are the perfect foil for creamy Greek yogurt. Try serving them with biscuits or brandy snaps for some crunch.

 2½ hours, plus cooling   4

- 600g/1lb 5oz ripe peaches, quartered and stoned
- juice 1 large orange
- 50g/2oz caster sugar
- 2 cinnamon sticks, broken
- 500g tub Greek yogurt
- zest 1 lemon

1 Heat the slow cooker if necessary. Stir the peaches, orange juice, sugar and cinnamon sticks into the slow-cooker pot. Cover and cook on Low for 1–2 hours until the peaches are tender. Remove the cinnamon and leave the peaches to cool.

2 Spoon the yogurt into a bowl and stir in the lemon zest, then fold in most of the cooled peaches. Spoon into four serving glasses and top with the remaining fruit and any juices.

· ·

PER SERVING 246 kcals, protein 9g, carbs 28g, fat 11g, sat fat 7g, fibre 3g, sugar 13g, salt 0.24g

Spiced poached pears in chocolate sauce

· · · · · · · · · · · · · · · · · · · ·

Don't waste the poaching syrup from the pears – freeze it to use another time, or to poach different fruit.

 4 hours, plus cooling (optional) 4

- 750g/1lb 10oz golden caster sugar
- 1 cinnamon stick
- 1 star anise
- 5 whole cloves
- 2 strips lemon zest (use a potato peeler)
- 1 vanilla pod, split lengthways
- knob ginger, peeled and sliced
- 4 ripe pears, peeled
- vanilla ice cream, to serve

FOR THE CHOCOLATE SAUCE

- 150ml/¼ pint each double cream and full-fat milk
- pinch ground cinnamon
- 200g/8oz good-quality dark chocolate, chopped

1 Heat the slow cooker if necessary. Tip in the sugar, spices, lemon zest, vanilla and ginger with 500ml/18fl oz boiling water. Cover and cook on High until the sugar has completely dissolved – about 15 minutes.

2 Add the pears, turn the heat to Low, replace the cover and cook for 2–3 hours until soft and tender – check by poking with a skewer or small knife. Turn off the heat. The pears can be kept in this syrup in the fridge for up to 2 days.

3 To make the sauce, bring the cream, milk and cinnamon to the boil. Take off the heat and stir in the chocolate until melted. To serve, drain the pears and, holding them by the stem, dip them in the chocolate sauce to cover completely. Serve each pear with a generous scoop of vanilla ice cream and any extra chocolate sauce on the side.

· ·

PER SERVING 642 kcals, protein 6g, carbs 66g, fat 41g, sat fat 22g, fibre 6g, sugar 58g, salt 0.08g

Poached apricots with rose water

The cooking time will vary slightly depending on the ripeness of the fruit, so keep an eye on these while cooking. Swap the apricots for peaches, if you feel like a change.

 2½ hours, plus cooling   2   Easily doubled

- 400g/14oz ripe apricots, halved and stoned
- 50g/2oz golden caster sugar
- few drops rose water
- Greek yogurt, to dollop
- handful pistachio nuts, roughly chopped, to scatter

1 Heat the slow cooker if necessary. Tip in the apricots, sprinkle over the sugar and splash over 100ml/3½fl oz water. Cover with the lid and cook on Low for 2 hours until soft.
2 Take off the heat, splash in the rose water an leave to cool. Spoon into glasses to serve, topped with a few dollops of the yogurt and a scattering of nuts.

PER SERVING 161 kcals, protein 2g, carbs 41g, fat none, sat fat none, fibre 3g, sugar 41g, salt 0.01g

Apple flapjack crumble

Sweetening the apples with apricot jam and orange juice makes this crumble twice as fruity.

 3 hours   6-8    Easily halved

- 1kg/2lb 4oz eating apples, peeled, cored and thinly sliced
- 3–4 tbsp apricot jam
- juice 1 large orange
- custard, ice cream or cream, to serve

FOR THE CRUMBLE
- 100g/4oz butter, melted
- 100g/4oz light muscovado sugar
- 1 tbsp golden syrup
- 140g/5oz porridge oats
- 100g/4oz plain flour
- 1 tsp ground cinnamon

1 Heat the slow cooker if necessary. Mix the apple slices with the jam and orange juice in the slow-cooker pot. Cook on Low for 2–4 hours until tender.

2 When the apples are nearly done, mix the crumble-topping ingredients in a large roasting tin. Heat grill to low and grill the crumble mix, stirring every 1–2 minutes, until golden and crisp.

3 When the apples are ready, transfer to a serving dish, or leave in the pot, if you like. Scatter with the crumble mix and eat with custard, ice cream or cream.

PER SERVING (6) 447 kcals, protein 6g, carbs 75g, fat 16g, sat fat 9g, fibre 6g, sugar 45g, salt 0.33g

Schooldays treacle sponge

Steamed sponges were made for slow cookers – just check your pudding basin fits in the cooking pot before you start assembling the pudding.

 5 hours  4 generously

- 175g/6oz unsalted butter, softened, plus extra for greasing
- 3 tbsp golden syrup, plus extra for drizzling (optional)
- 1 tbsp fresh white breadcrumbs
- 175g/6oz golden caster sugar
- zest 1 lemon
- 3 eggs, beaten
- 175g/6oz self-raising flour
- 2 tbsp milk
- custard or clotted cream, to serve

1 Heat the slow cooker if necessary. Use a small knob of butter heavily to grease a 1-litre pudding basin. In a small bowl, mix the golden syrup with the breadcrumbs, then tip into the pudding basin.

2 Beat the butter with the sugar and zest until light and fluffy, then add the eggs gradually. Fold in the flour, then finally add the milk.

3 Spoon the mix into the pudding basin. Cover with a double layer of buttered foil and baking paper, making a pleat in the centre to allow the pudding to rise. Tie the foil securely with string, then put in the slow-cooker pot, pouring in enough boiling water from the kettle to come halfway up the sides of the basin. Cover with the lid and cook on High for 4 hours until a skewer poked in the centre of the pudding comes out clean.

4 Turn out the pudding on to a serving dish. Serve with lashings of custard or clotted cream and a little extra golden syrup drizzled over, if you wish.

PER SERVING 763 kcals, protein 10g, carbs 90g, fat 43g, sat fat 25g, fibre 1g, sugar 56g, salt 0.71g

Blackberry queen of pudding pots

These puddings are perfect if you have a glut of blackberries. If using wild fruits, tast
a few first, gauge how sweet they are, then add more sugar accordingly.

 2 hours 3

- 1 tbsp butter, plus extra for greasing
- 300ml/½ pint full-fat milk
- zest ½ lemon
- 2 eggs, separated
- 100g/4oz golden caster sugar
- 2 individual brioche rolls, sliced
- 75g/2½oz blackberry jam or bramble jelly
- 200g/8oz blackberries

1 Grease three large individual ramekins (about 300ml each), first checking they can fit in your slow cooker. Heat the slow cooker necessary. Bring the milk, lemon zest and butter to the boil in a pan, then turn off the heat. Beat the egg yolks with half of the sugar, then strain the hot milk over the sugar egg yolks, beating constantly.

2 Push the brioche into the ramekins so they a half-full. Pour the custard equally over the brioche, cover the ramekins with foil and pu in the slow-cooker pot. Pour in enough boilin water to come halfway up the sides of the ramekins. Cover and cook for 1 hour on High until the custard is set, then remove the ramekins from the slow cooker. Mix the jam with the berries, mashing them a little, and divide among the ramekins.

3 Heat grill to medium. Whisk the egg whites to stiff peaks, then gradually whisk in the remaining sugar until stiff again. Swirl meringue over each, then grill until golden.

PER PUDDING 493 kcals, protein 12g, carbs 78g, fat 17g, sat fat 8g, fibre 3g, sugar 63g, salt 0.68g

Self-saucing Jaffa pudding

· ·

This pud starts life as an ugly duckling, but don't fear as the hot, watery sauce floats among the batter – once you bake it, you'll end up with something beautiful.

 4 hours   8

- 100g/4oz butter, melted, plus a little extra for greasing
- 250g/9oz self-raising flour
- 140g/5oz caster sugar
- 50g/2oz cocoa powder
- 1 tsp baking powder
- zest and juice 1 orange
- 3 eggs
- 150ml/¼ pint milk
- 100g/4oz orange milk chocolate or milk chocolate, broken into chunks
- vanilla ice cream or single cream, to serve

FOR THE SAUCE

- 200g/8oz light muscovado sugar
- 25g/1oz cocoa powder

1 Heat the slow cooker, if necessary. Butter the slow-cooker pot. Put the flour, caster sugar, cocoa, baking powder, orange zest and a pinch of salt in a large mixing bowl. Whisk together the orange juice and any pulp left in the juicer, the eggs, melted butter and milk, then pour on to the dry ingredients, and mix together until smooth. Stir in the chocolate chunks and scrape everything into the slow-cooker pot.

2 Mix 300ml/½ pint boiling water from the kettle with the sugar and cocoa for the sauce, then pour this all over the pudding batter – don't worry, it will look very strange at this stage! Return the pot to the slow-cooker base, cover and cook on High for 3 hours until the surface looks firm and risen. As you scoop spoonfuls, you should find a rich chocolate sauce underneath the sponge. Eat immediately with vanilla ice cream or single cream.

· ·

PER SERVING 522 kcals, protein 8g, carbs 82g, fat 21g, sat fat 11g, fibre 2g, sugar 54g, salt 0.86g

Roast apples with cinnamon sugar

Baked apples are the perfect pudding when it's cold outside. Eat these with hot custard, ice cream or single cream.

 4 hours   6   Easily halved

- 50g/2oz natural dried breadcrumbs
- 8 dried apricots, roughly chopped
- 75g/2½oz sugar
- 1 tsp ground cinnamon
- 75g/2½oz butter, chopped
- zest and juice 1 orange
- 6 large Bramley apples
- custard, ice cream or single cream, to serve

1 Heat the slow cooker if necessary. Mix together the breadcrumbs, apricots, sugar, cinnamon, butter and orange zest to make the filling. Set aside.

2 Using an apple corer, remove the centre of each apple, then score the skin across the equator so that they don't collapse during cooking.

3 Pack the filling into the apples, then sit them snugly in the slow-cooker pot. Mix together the orange juice and 100ml/3½fl oz water, and pour round the apples. Cover and cook on Low for 2–3 hours until the apples are tender. Serve with the pot juices and custard ice cream or single cream.

. . . .
PER SERVING 246 kcals, protein 2g, carbs 38g, fat 11g, sat fat 7g, fibre 3g, sugar 32g, salt 0.26g

Baked raspberry & bramble trifle

This wonderful make-ahead pudding is loosely based on a traditional trifle, but with the added twist of a layer of creamy baked custard.

 6 hours, plus overnight chilling 4–6

- 200g/8oz raspberries, fresh or frozen, plus extra to decorate
- 140g/5oz shop-bought Madeira cake or any other light sponge, thinly sliced
- 3 tbsp sherry
- grated zest and juice 1 small orange
- 500ml/18fl oz double cream
- 2 eggs
- 50g/2oz golden caster sugar
- few drops vanilla extract
- 4 tbsp bramble jam or jelly
- 3 shop-bought shortbread biscuits, coarsely crumbled
- icing sugar, to dust

1 Layer the raspberries and cake in a deep heatproof dish that will fit in your slow cooker. Spoon over the sherry and orange juice.

2 Heat the slow cooker if necessary. Whisk together 400ml/14fl oz of the double cream with the eggs, sugar, orange zest and vanilla extract to make a custard. Spread the jam over the sponge and fruit to cover completely, then slowly pour on the custard mixture. Cover with foil, sit in the slow cooker pot and pour in enough boiling water from the kettle to come halfway up the sides of the dish. Cover and cook on High for 4 hours until the custard is just set with a little wobble. Cool, then cover and chill overnight.

3 To serve, whip the remaining cream until it just holds its shape, then spoon over the custard. Scatter over the extra raspberries and the shortbread, and finish with a dusting of icing sugar.

PER SERVING (4) 873 kcals, protein 9g, carbs 53g, fat 70g, sat fat 42g, fibre 2g, sugar 36g, salt 0.58g

Nectarine & raspberry gratin

Nectarines are easily swapped for peaches or plums in this recipe, and if fresh raspberries aren't available, frozen work fine too.

 1½ hours   4

- 4 very ripe nectarines, halved and stoned
- 150g punnet raspberries
- 150ml pot double cream
- 50g/2oz demerara sugar
- icing sugar or cocoa powder, sifted, for dusting

1 Heat the slow cooker if necessary. Sprinkle the base of the slow-cooker pot with a little water, then sit in the nectarines, cut-side down. Cover and cook for 1 hour on Medium until tender but not falling apart. Transfer to individual gratin dishes, or one large baking dish, cut-side up. Chill until just before ready to serve.

2 Heat grill to medium. Pile the raspberries in the centre of each nectarine half. Drizzle cream over the fruit, sprinkle with sugar, then grill for 8–10 minutes until bubbling and golden. Dust with icing sugar or cocoa and serve.

PER SERVING 309 kcals, protein 3g, carbs 30g, fat 20g, sat fat 11g, fibre 3g, sugar 13, salt 0.04g

Summer compote

This is equally delicious served hot or chilled. You need at least two of the fruits suggested here, but you can use more, if you wish.

🕐 1 hour 10 minutes   🥧 4   🌓 Easily halved or doubled

- 500g/1lb 2oz mixed berries (blackcurrants, blueberries, raspberries, redcurrants, strawberries)
- 50g/2oz golden caster sugar
- 1 vanilla pod or cinnamon stick
- 2–3 mint or lemon balm sprigs (optional)
- Ice cream, to serve

1 Heat the slow cooker if necessary. Tip all the fruits into the slow-cooker pot (if using strawberries, leave these to one side) with the sugar, vanilla pod or cinnamon stick and herbs, if using. Cover and cook for 1 hour on High.

2 Throw in the strawberries, if using, and cook for 20 minutes more. Once cool, this keeps in the fridge for up to 2 days; in the freezer for up to 3 months.

PER SERVING 83 kcals, protein 1g, carbs 20g, fat none, sat fat none, fibre 3g, sugar 13g, salt 0.01g

Sloe mulled wine

Slow cookers are ideal for making this classic winter warmer, also delicious in mulled fruit puddings or for soaking vine fruits for a luxury Christmas pud.

 2–4 hours 6 Easily doubled

- 750ml bottle red wine
- 1 large cinnamon stick or 2 small ones
- 2 star anise
- 4 whole cloves
- 2 strips lemon zest, pared using a vegetable peeler
- 4 tbsp caster sugar
- 100ml/3½fl oz sloe gin

1 Heat the slow cooker if necessary. Mix all the ingredients together in the slow-cooker pot then cover and cook on High for 2 hours, or 4 hours on Low.
2 Ladle into mugs or glasses to serve, and leave the slow cooker on Low with the lid off to keep the wine warm.

PER SERVING 168 kcals, protein none, carbs 16g, fat none, sat fat none, fibre none, sugar 16g, salt 0.03

Spicy plum & apple chutney

This chutney is so versatile it won't last long. Eat with cold meats, cheese sandwiches or as an alternative to mango chutney with poppadums.

🕐 5-6 hours 📖 4-5 jars

- 1 garlic bulb, cloves separated, peeled and sliced
- thumb-sized knob ginger, peeled and thinly shredded
- 2 large onions, thinly sliced
- 1kg/2lb 4oz Bramley apples, peeled, cored and chopped
- 3 star anise
- 1 tsp cumin seeds
- 1 cinnamon stick
- 200g/8oz golden caster sugar
- 1kg/2lb 4oz plums, stoned and quartered
- 250ml/9fl oz cider vinegar

1 Heat the slow cooker if necessary. Mix together the garlic, ginger, onions, apples, star anise, cumin seeds, cinnamon, sugar and 1 tablespoon salt in the slow-cooker pot. Cover and cook for 2 hours on High until the apples are tender.

2 Stir in the plums and vinegar, cover and cook for another 2–3 hours on High until pulpy. Stir the chutney every now and then while it's cooking.

3 Discard the cinnamon stick and star anise before ladling the chutney into sterilised jars.

PER TBSP 38 kcals, protein none, carbs 10g, fat none, sat fat none, fibre 1g, sugar 9g, salt 0.22g

Onion, orange & coriander confit

Transform an abundant batch of onions into this moreish preserve to serve with cheese or cold meats, or stir it into casseroles and sauces.

 4½ hours    3–4 jars

- 1kg/2lb 4oz onions
- 1 large orange
- 2 tbsp olive oil
- 50g/2oz butter
- 1 tbsp coriander seeds, coarsely crushed
- 1 tsp black peppercorns, coarsely crushed
- 2 tsp sea salt
- 140g/5oz light muscovado sugar
- 150ml/¼ pint red wine vinegar
- 2 tbsp balsamic vinegar

1 Heat the slow cooker. Thinly slice the onions (you can do this with the slicing blade of the food processor, if you have one). Thinly slice the orange, then cut each slice into quarters.

2 Heat the oil and butter in a pan. Add the coriander seeds and peppercorns, and fry until they start to smell fragrant. Add the onions and gently fry, stirring, until they start to colour, about 10 minutes. Scoop everything into the slow-cooker pot and add the remaining ingredients. Cook for 4 hours, stirring occasionally until thick and pulpy.

3 Heat the oven to 160C/140C fan/gas 3. Now sterilise the jars; washing them in hot soapy water and rinsing well. Boil vinegar-proof lids for 5 minutes and leave to dry. Put the jars upright in a roasting tin in the oven for 15 minutes.

4 Remove the jars and set on a board. Fill with the onion confit and screw on the lids. Label and store in a cool, dry place for 2 weeks to allow the flavours to develop. Will keep for up to 6 months.

PER TBSP 23 kcals, protein none, carbs 3g, fat 1g, sat fat none, fibre none, sugar 3g, salt 0.2g

Lemon curd

· ·

Enjoy this zesty lemon curd spread over scones or toast, or use it to sandwich together the layers of a Victoria sponge.

🕐 3½ hours   📑 1 jar

- 50g/2oz melted butter
- 175g/6oz caster sugar
- zest and juice 2 lemons
- 3 eggs, beaten

1 Heat the slow cooker if necessary. Mix the butter, sugar and lemon juice in a small heatproof bowl that will fit inside your slow cooker. Add the eggs to the bowl and give everything a stir.

2 Put the bowl into the slow cooker and cover with foil. Add a string handle to help you lift it. Pour in hot water from the kettle until it comes halfway up the sides of the bowl.

3 Cover and cook on Low for 2–3 hours – the mixture should be set at the edges, but still runny in the centre. Remove and whisk until the mixture is an even thickness and smooth, then push through a fine sieve. Stir in the zest and spoon into a sterilised jar, if not cooling and using immediately. Will keep in the fridge for up to 3 weeks.

· ·

PER TBSP 112 kcals, protein 2g, carbs 15g, fat 5g, sat fat 3g, fibre none, sugar 15g, salt 0.11g

Seville orange marmalade

Buy Seville oranges as soon as you see them in the shops as the season is very short. You can always throw them in the freezer, then defrost them when you have time.

🕐 9–11 hours, plus overnight cooling 🥧 8 x 450g/1lb jars

- 1kg/2lb 4oz Seville oranges, well scrubbed and halved
- juice 1 lemon
- 2kg/4lb 8oz granulated sugar

1 Heat the slow cooker if necessary and put a saucer in the freezer. Put the oranges in the slow-cooker pot, cover with boiling water and top with a second upturned saucer to stop them floating. Cover and cook on Low for 8–10 hours. Leave to cool in the pot overnight.

2 The next day, lift the oranges out of the pot, but don't discard the liquid. Quarter the oranges, scoop out and discard the pips, then thinly slice the quarters.

3 Put the orange slices, cooking liquid, lemon juice and sugar in a very large, wide pan. Gently heat until the sugar has dissolved, the simmer for 20 minutes. Spoon a blob of marmalade on to the cold saucer. Leave for a few seconds, then push the marmalade with your finger. If it wrinkles, it's ready. If not, boil for 10 minutes more then try again (it can take up to 45 minutes).

4 Once you've reached setting point, ladle the marmalade into warm, sterilised jars and sea

PER TBSP 57 kcals, protein none, carbs 15g, fat none, sat fat none, fibre none, sugar 15g, salt none

Index

lso available from BBC Books and Good Food